how to build
WORKBENCHES
TOOL CHESTS

Donald R. Brann

SEVENTH PRINTING — 1979

REVISED EDITION

Published by
DIRECTIONS SIMPLIFIED, INC.

Division of
EASI-BILD PATTERN CO., INC.
Briarcliff Manor, NY 10510

Library of Congress Card No. 66-30452

There's Magic
in Movement

Nature continually tries to show us better ways to live. Watch a bee buzz a flower, search and find honey, a gull plunge from above and come up with a mouthful of fish, and you realize there's a lot of magic in movement. Everything the eye can see, and much more too small to discern, is continually active. Nothing remains motionless.

The mind, like other particles of microscopic matter, is also in constant motion. It views each happening from many different angles. A problem will plunge us into motionless despair, then pass. Continually buffeted by thoughts, sights and feelings over which we have little control, all too often we neglect to keep moving, keep trying to find a solution. The minutes, hours, days and weeks we spend worrying about situations that may or may not happen, or have occurred, consume a substantial part of our inheritance of time. Since time is our most precious possession, learning to refocus one's mentalens is vitally important to good health. Keep busy doing something that requires physical and mental effort. Allow time and the magic of movement to carry you through.

Don Brann

TABLE OF CONTENTS

17 — 6' Workbench

27 — Child's Size Bench

30 — Foldaway Workbench

50 — Table Top Workbench

64 — Sawhorse Tool Chest

72 — Power Tool Workshop

75 — Grinder and Storage Drawer Cabinet

84 — Sawhorse Storage Cabinet

86 — Storage Cabinet and Tote Box

92 — Corner Workbench

102 — Radial Arm Saw Bench

110 — Wall Cabinet with Revolving Tool Turret

116 — Corner Unit

119 — Lumber Rack on Casters

121 — 6 Drawer Workbench with 6' Vise

139 — Swedish Door Chimes

149 — Tool Chest

158 — Metric Conversion Chart

160 — Cross Reference Index

174 — Other Books by Author

176 — Lumber Chart

177 — Screw Chart

178 — Nail Chart

179 — Full Size Foldout Pattern

180 — Carpentry Tips

Opportunity still knocks

Those who appreciate the importance of change realize opportunity continually knocks for those willing to listen. This book is a case in point. It explains how to build a workbench that will simplify making home repairs and improvements. It also explains how to start a part or full time business with no capital investment. Building a bench to fill your own needs offers proof of your ability to build, plus a sample that can help cultivate sales to others.

Today's excessive cost of shipping nurtures many new business opportunities. Because of size and weight, a workbench costs a bundle to ship from manufacturer to retailer to customer. Buying material from a local lumber yard, selling workbenches to those willing to pick it up, offers sizeable savings to all concerned. It's especially attractive to those wishing to contribute to a church, charity or other fund raising drive. When the benches, cabinets, sawhorse and wall tool chest are sold at a charity sponsored auction, each attracts top dollar plus very satisfied buyers.

Those interested in setting up a power tool workshop will find the base and wall cabinets designed especially for a radial arm saw, grinder and other tools a practical solution to a costly problem. Directions also explain how to build a corner workbench, rolling lumber cart, tote box, sawhorse tool chest, workshop storage cabinets, plus other projects. Base cabinets can be built to size space permits then covered with a one piece countertop.

6 DRAWER WORKBENCH WITH 6' VISE

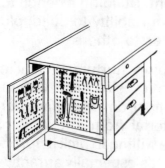

STORES HAND TOOLS

VISE HOLDS LARGE PANELS

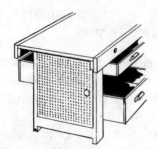

DRAWERS OPEN FROM BOTH SIDES

6 FT. WORKBENCH

CHILD'S SIZE BENCH

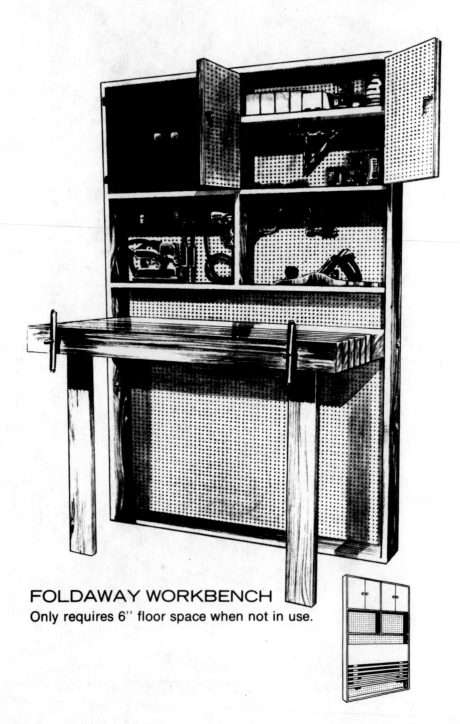

FOLDAWAY WORKBENCH

Only requires 6'' floor space when not in use.

**FULL WIDTH VISE
HOLDS LARGE PANELS**

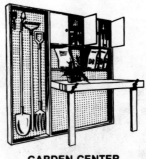

GARDEN CENTER

SEWING CENTER

**BENCH CAN BE LOWERED
FOR JUNIOR CRAFTSMEN**

TRAIN TABLE

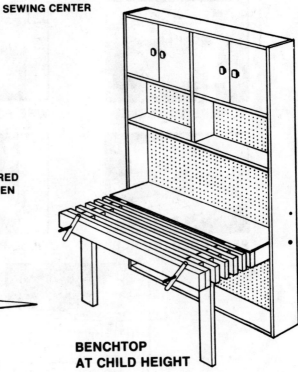

**BENCHTOP
AT CHILD HEIGHT**

11

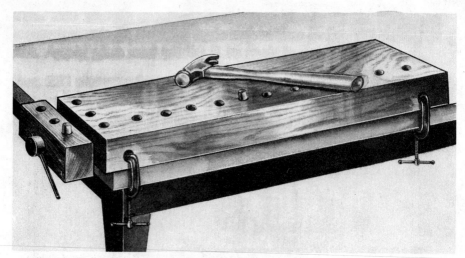

TABLE TOP WORKBENCH

"MULTI-USE"

CLAMPS TO TABLE

VISE FOR SAWING

PEGS HOLD BOARDS

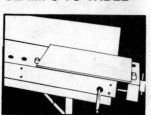

GLUE BOARDS

CLAMP FOR PLANING

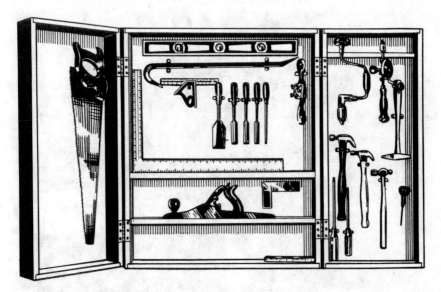

TOOL CHEST STORAGE

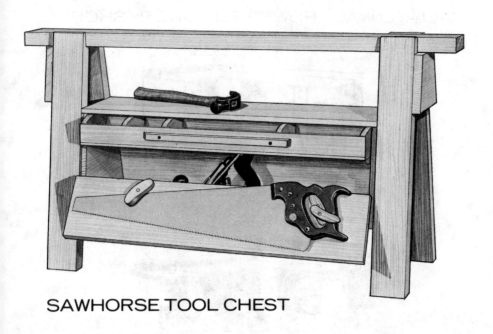

SAWHORSE TOOL CHEST

13

WALL-TO-WALL POWER TOOL WORKSHOP

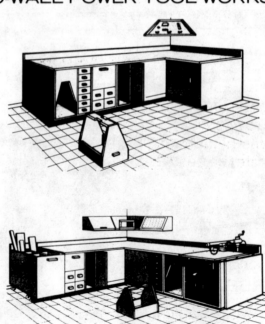

SWEDISH DOOR CHIMES

Building and selling workbenches is a fun way to earn money. While this book simplifies construction of many types, the six drawer bench, Illus. 165, is very popular with knowledgeable craftsmen. Through an ingenious, yet simple method of construction, this bench offers two six foot vises, one along each edge. Two perforated hardboard doors, enclosing end compartments, provide truly convenient storage for hand tools. The big drawers have handles on both sides. This provides step saving, easily accessible storage. Sturdy in construction, this bench is considered tops by all who appreciate the best. Step by step construction starts on page 121.

The child size workbench, built to size suggested, has considerable appeal. Having a place to work encourages a youngster to develop a hobby. If bench top is too high for your child, build a platform, Illus. 16. This raises the child 4''.

Building the projects offered not only provides an economical solution to a problem, but also hours of escape and relaxation.

Step by step directions simplify building every type of workbench from a 6' adult bench to a child size. Each can be constructed to size suggested or lengthened to size desired.

Due to variance in lumber width and thickness, always cut inner framing members to length assembled parts require. Always drill holes in one part then use it to locate position of hole in adjoining part. For example: After drilling holes in leg A, place it in position against E. Use an 8 or 10 penny nail to locate and drill hole in E.

The table top bench is of special inerest to every craftsman. It's ideal for the hobby minded youngster who may prefer working in a bedroom.

The foldaway bench was designed to serve every spare time interest from woodworking, jewelry making, ceramics, model railroading to sewing and gardening. When closed, it only requires 6" of floor space.

NOTE: For greater strength and rigidity, apply glue to all permanent wood-to-wood joints. Dip screws in glue before driving. Wipe away excess glue with a damp rag before it's allowed to set.

Always select straight lengths of kiln dried lumber, surfaced four sides (S4S). If lumber has small tight knots, paint knots with glue.

We figured surfaced lumber as measuring:

1 x 2 — ¾ x 1½"
1 x 3 — ¾ x 2½"
1 x 4 — ¾ x 3½"
1 x 6 — ¾ x 5½"
1 x 8 — ¾ x 7¼"
2 x 4 — 1½ x 3½"
2 x 6 — 1½ x 5½"
5/4" lumber — 1-1/16

Read directions completely before cutting any parts.

6' WORKBENCH

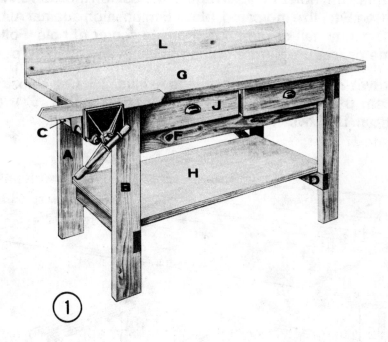

①

LIST OF MATERIALS

3 — 2 x 6 x 12' A,B,G
1 — 2 x 6 x 10' A,C,E
1 — 2 x 6 x 5' C,B
1 — 2 x 4 x 10' D,F
1 — 1 x 6 x 12' L,K
1 — 1 x 6 x 10' K,J
1 — 1 x 8 x 4' M,N,O,P
1 — ¾ x 24 x 51" plywood, H
1 — ¼ x 24 x 40" plywood, Q
60 — 1" No. 8 flathead wood screws
24 — 1½" No. 10   ''   ''   ''
16 — 2" No. 10   ''   ''   ''
 9 — 2½" No. 10   ''   ''   ''
20 — 2¾" No. 12   ''   ''   ''
16 — 3" No. 14   ''   ''   ''
6 — ⅜ x 4" carriage bolts, washers, nuts
2 — drawer pulls

17

NOTE: To simplify drilling holes in exact position required, do this. Drill holes in legs A and B, in position indicated. After cutting E to size indicated, place E in position against A. Use a 10 penny nail or punch to indicate center of hole. Follow same procedure before drilling holes in all adjoining parts.

Cut two 2 x 6 x 39" for back legs A, Illus. 2,3. Cut 1½ x 5½" notch, 6⅝" from top end. Cut 1½ x 3½" notch, 5" from bottom. Drill two ⅜" holes (e) in position indicated.

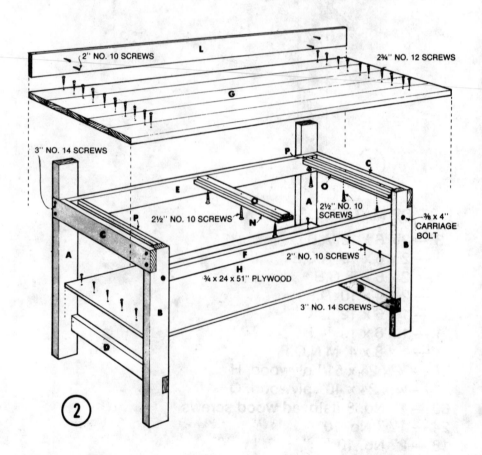

2" NO. 10 SCREWS
L
2¾" NO. 12 SCREWS
G
3" NO. 14 SCREWS
P
C
E
O
A
2½" NO. 10 SCREWS
Q
2½" NO. 10 SCREWS
N
⅜ x 4" CARRIAGE BOLT
C
A
F
2" NO. 10 SCREWS
B
H
¾ x 24 x 51" PLYWOOD
B
D
D
3" NO. 14 SCREWS

(2)

Cut two 2 x 6 x 32⅜" for legs B, Illus. 2,4. Drill ⅜" hole at (f), Illus. 4. Cut 1½ x 5½" and 1½ x 3½" notches in position indicated.

18

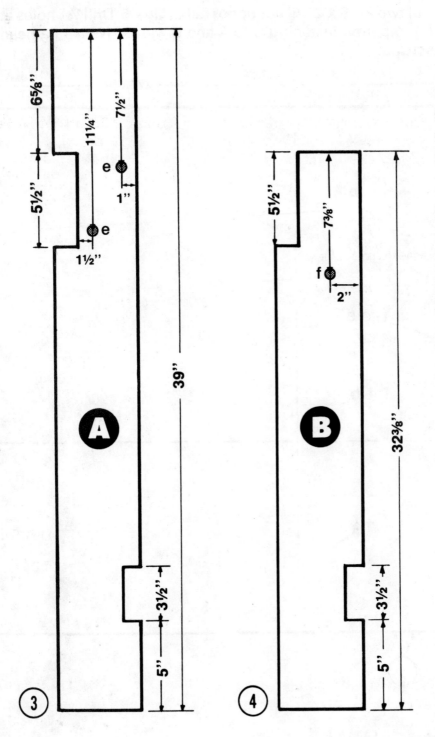

Cut two 2 x 6 x 27¼" for upper rail C, Illus. 5. Drill ¼" holes at
(a) to permit fastening C to A and B with 3" No. 14 flathead
screws.

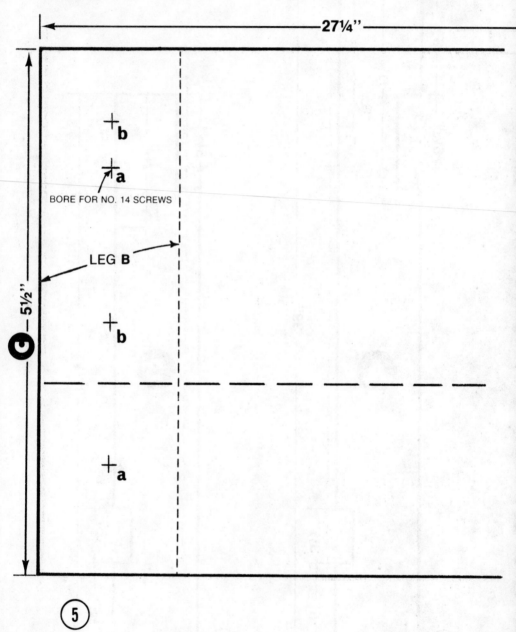

20

Cut two 2 x 4 x 27¼" for lower side rail D, Illus. 2, 5. Bore four holes for No. 14 screws where indicated at (b).

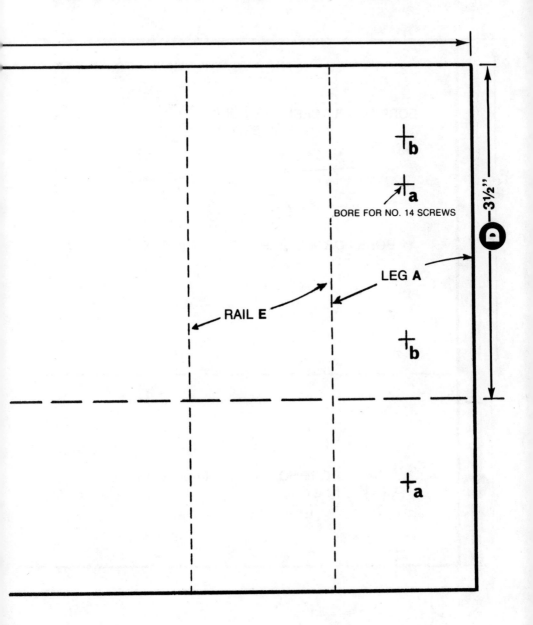

BORE FOR NO. 14 SCREWS

LEG **A**

RAIL **E**

D

—3½"

Cut one 2 x 6 x 51" for upper back rail E, Illus. 6. Place leg A in position, Illus. 2. Locate and drill two ⅜" holes (e), Illus. 3.

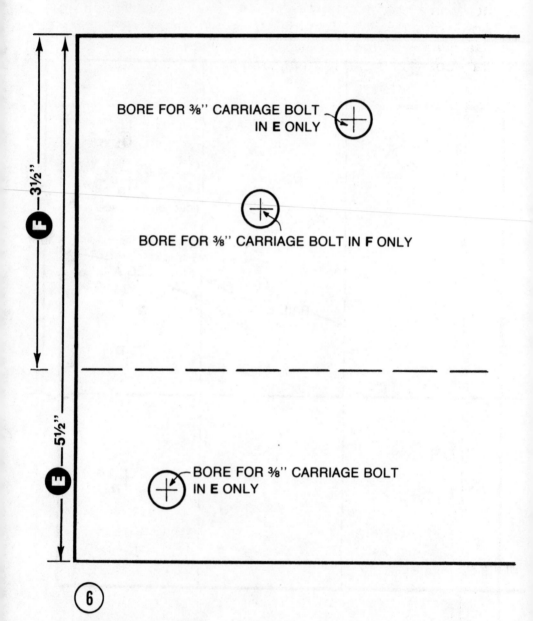

BORE FOR ⅜" CARRIAGE BOLT IN **E** ONLY

BORE FOR ⅜" CARRIAGE BOLT IN **F** ONLY

BORE FOR ⅜" CARRIAGE BOLT IN **E** ONLY

⑥

Cut one 2 x 4 x 51" for upper front rail F, Illus. 6. Place leg B in position, Illus. 2. Locate and drill one ⅜" hole where indicated (f), Illus. 3.

Cut five 2 x 6 x 72" for top G, Illus. 7. Drill 7/32" holes at (g) in four boards to receive 2¾"No.12 flathead screws. Don't drill holes in front board until you are ready to assemble top. Apply glue to edge when ready to assemble top. Or you can use two ¾ x 28 x 72" panels of flakeboard, or one ¾" flakeboard and one ¼" tempered hardboard for top.

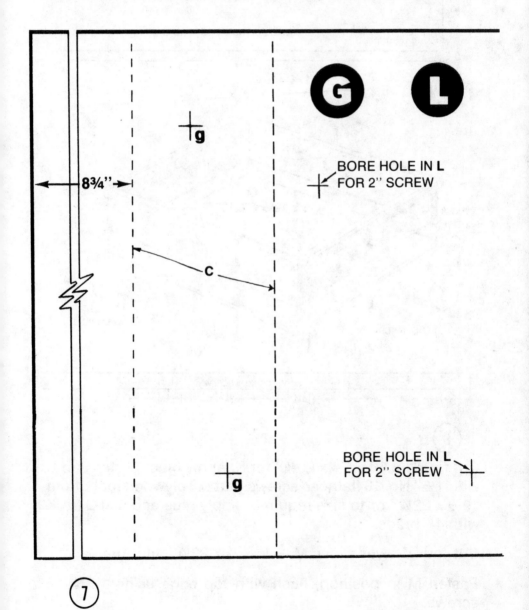

G L

8¾"

BORE HOLE IN **L** FOR 2" SCREW

C

BORE HOLE IN **L** FOR 2" SCREW

7

Cut ¾ x 24 x 51" plywood for shelf H, Illus. 2.

Cut four 1 x 6 to 5¼ x 19½" for J, Illus. 8,9.

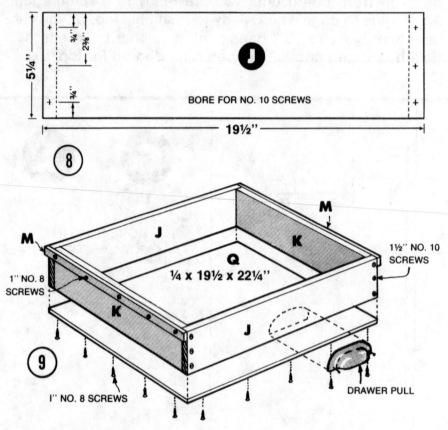

Cut four 1 x 6 to 5¼ x 20¾" for K. Apply glue. Fasten J to K with 1½" No. 10 flathead screws. Cut ¼" plywood for bottom 19½ x 22¼" or to size required. Apply glue and nail Q to JK with 1" brads.

Cut four drawer slides M — ½ x ¾ x 22¼", Illus. 9a.

Fasten M in position, flush with top edge using 1" No. 8 screws.

24

Cut one 1 x 6 x 72" for fence L, Illus. 2,7.

Cut one drawer hanger N — ¾ x 2⅝ x 22¼", Illus. 2,10,14.

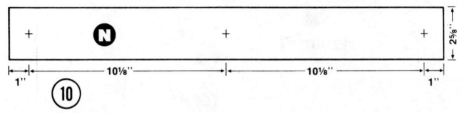

Cut three drawer hanger strips O — ¾ x 1⅝ x 22¼", Illus. 2,11,14.

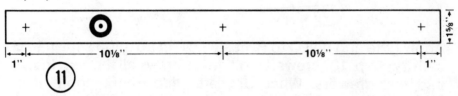

Cut two drawer hanger strips P — ¾ x 1¼ x 22¼", Illus. 12.

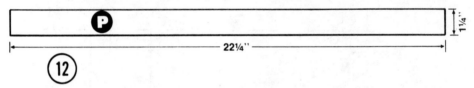

ASSEMBLY — Apply glue to all permanent wood-to-wood contacts. Fasten rail C and D to legs A and B, Illus. 2, with 3" No. 14 screws.

Drill holes to countersink shank on Teenut, Illus. 13. Drive Teenut in position following manufacturer's directions. Bolt A to E with four ⅜ x 4" slotted head stove bolts with Teenuts, or use ⅜ x 4" carriage bolts, washers and nuts. Fasten shelf H to D with 2" No. 10 screws.

Apply glue to top edge of C. Screw G to C in position shown with 2¾" No. 12 screws. Screw fence L to A with 2" No. 10 screws.

Turn bench over. Draw center line on bottom of G, Illus. 14.

Glue and nail O to N with 1" brads. Drill holes and fasten O and N temporarily in position to G. Don't use glue.

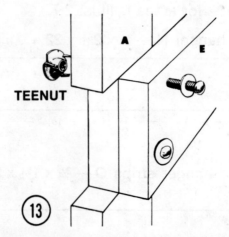

TEENUT

(13)

Apply glue and nail O to P. Fasten OP in position shown to G with 2½" No. 10 screws. Don't drive screws all the way. Install and test drawers. When drawers slide freely, apply glue, fasten ON and OP permanently in position.

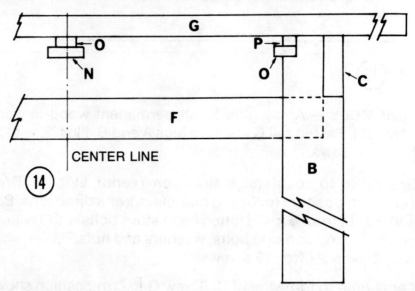

(14)

If bench is to be subjected to heavy work, additional rigidity can be built in by fastening a 1 x 3 diagonal brace from back of B to front of A.

A 4 x 9" woodworkers vise can be fastened to left front end of completed bench. Apply drawer pulls to drawers. Countersink all screw heads and fill holes with wood filler.

CHILD'S SIZE BENCH

LIST OF MATERIALS
1 — 2 x 3 x 10' R,S, or use 2 x 4
1 — 1 x 4 x 6' U
1 — 1 x 4 x 8' T,X
1 — ¾ x 26 x 31" plywood, V,W
8 — ⅜ x 3" carriage bolts, washers and nuts*
42 — 1¾" No. 9 screws

Cut 1 x 4 to 1 x 3

While this list permits building a child's size bench, Illus. 15, measuring 31" long, 14" deep, with bench top approximately 25¾" from floor, legs can be cut any height desired. Since a growing child will use a workbench for years, we suggest building to height specified, even if it requires building a platform to stand on. The platform can be built with two 2 x 4 on edge, plus a ½" top, Illus. 16. This will raise child 4". Build platform approximately 2 x 3' or size desired.

*or 8 — ⅜ x 2½" cap screws or round head stove bolts, and 8 — ⅜" Teenuts.   27

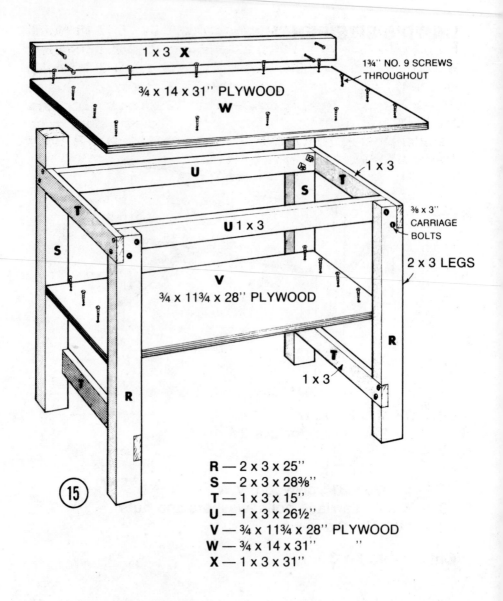

1 x 3 **X**

1¾" NO. 9 SCREWS
THROUGHOUT

¾ x 14 x 31" PLYWOOD
W

U

1 x 3

S

T

U 1 x 3

T

S

⅜ x 3"
CARRIAGE
BOLTS

2 x 3 LEGS

V
¾ x 11¾ x 28" PLYWOOD

R

T

1 x 3

V

R

⑮

R — 2 x 3 x 25"
S — 2 x 3 x 28⅜"
T — 1 x 3 x 15"
U — 1 x 3 x 26½"
V — ¾ x 11¾ x 28" PLYWOOD
W — ¾ x 14 x 31"
X — 1 x 3 x 31"

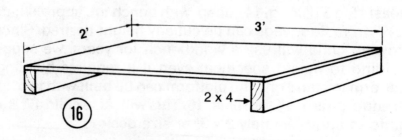

2'

3'

2 x 4

⑯

Cut all parts of bench to size indicated, Illus. 15,17,18. Notch R and S to receive T. When assembling, glue all permanent wood-to-wood contacts. Screw T to R and S. Drill ⅜" holes and bolt U to R and S. Screw V to T. Screw W to T and U. Screw X to S. If desired, drawers can be added by following procedure used for adult size bench. If drawers are to be installed, fasten front rail U 5" down from top of leg R. Build drawers to fit smaller bench.

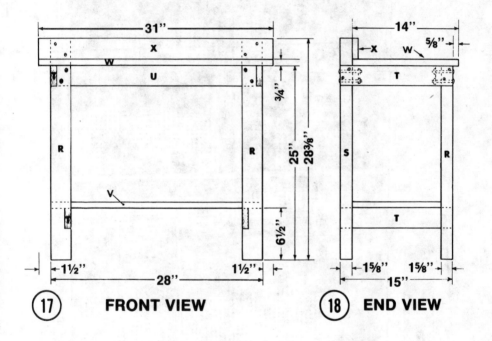

⑰ **FRONT VIEW**   ⑱ **END VIEW**

FOLDAWAY WORKBENCH

LIST OF MATERIALS

1 x 6 — 2/8', 2/10', A,B,C,D,E,F
1 x 2 — 2/10', H,J,T,U
5/4 x 4 — 4/8',1/12',1/6', K,M,N,R,Q
5/4 x 2 — 1/4', L
1 — ⅛" x 4 x 8' pegboard, G,W
1 — ⅛" x 3 x 4' hardboard, P,V
1 — 3' length of ½" threaded steel rod, four nuts and washers
4 — 2 x 2" loose pin butt hinges with screws
4 — door pulls
4 — plunger type cabinet catches
4 — 2 x 2" angle irons with screws
2 — ½ x 3" carriage bolts with washers and wing nuts
16" of 1" aluminum tubing
18" – ⅞" dowel
¼ lb. 8 penny finishing nails
½ lb. 6   ''   ''   ''
2 lbs. 4   ''   ''   ''
1 box ¾" brads
1 box ¾" wire nails
Glue

Cut two sides A — 1 x 6 x 72", Illus. 20. Bore ½" holes where noted, Illus. 21, 31¾" from bottom for an adult size bench, 27½" for child.

Cut two B, two C — 1 x 6 x 46½". Apply glue and nail A to B with 6 penny finishing nails, Illus. 22. Glue and nail A to C, Illus. 23, in position noted, Illus. 20.

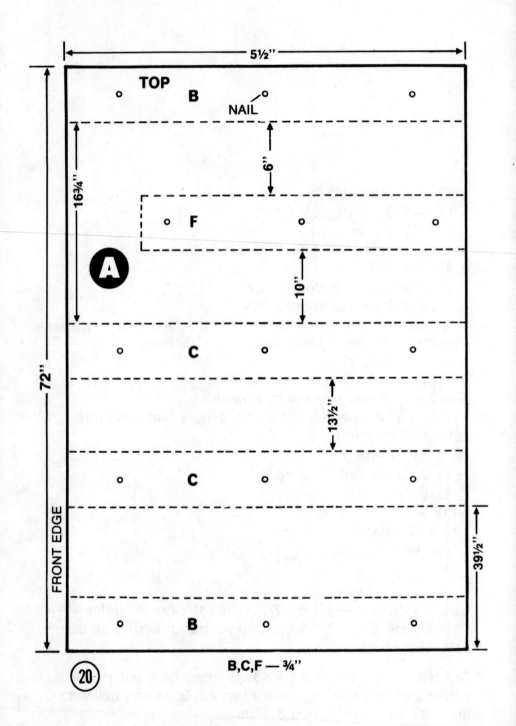

TOP

B

NAIL

5½"

16¾"

6"

F

A

10"

C

13½"

C

39½"

72"

FRONT EDGE

B

B,C,F — ¾"

20

32

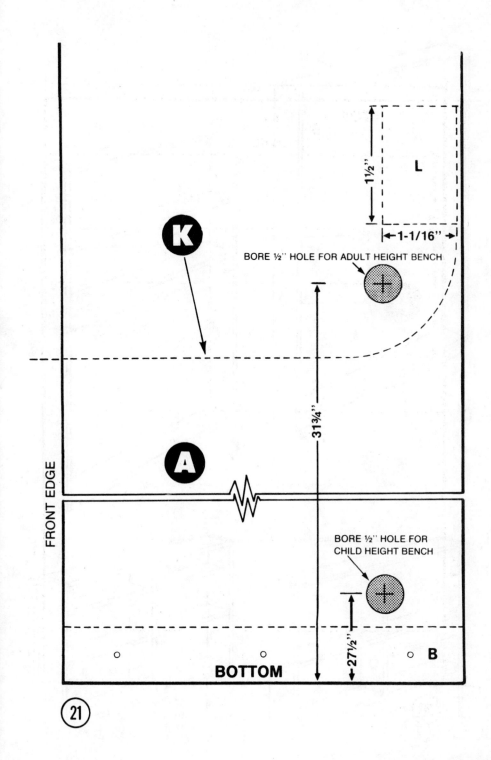

1½"

L

1-1/16"

K

BORE ½" HOLE FOR ADULT HEIGHT BENCH

31¾"

FRONT EDGE

A

BORE ½" HOLE FOR
CHILD HEIGHT BENCH

27½"

BOTTOM

B

㉑

33

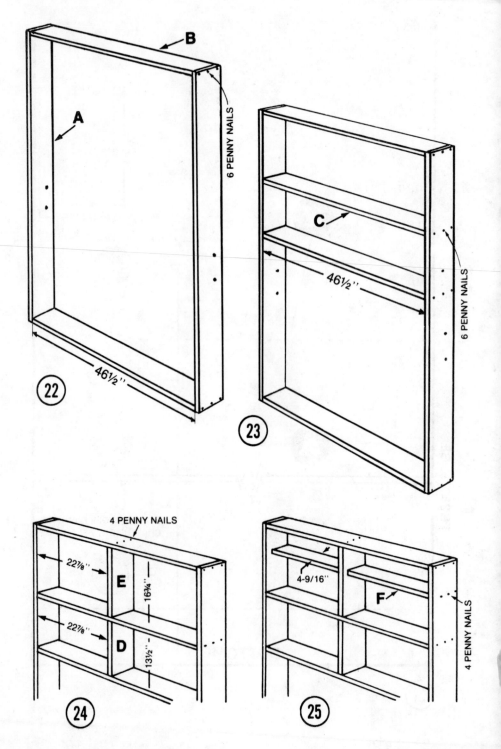

22
A
B
6 PENNY NAILS
46½"

23
C
46½"
6 PENNY NAILS

24
4 PENNY NAILS
22⅞"
22⅞"
E
D
16¾"
13½"

25
4-9/16"
F
4 PENNY NAILS

Cut D — 1 x 6 x 13½"; E — 1 x 6 x 16¾", Illus. 24, or to length required. Glue and nail D, then E in position with 4 penny finishing nails. Nail through B into E, toenail E to C.

Cut two F — 4-9/16 x 22⅞" from 1 x 6. Glue and nail F in position, Illus. 20,25.

Cut back G — 4'0" x 6'0" from ⅛" pegboard, Illus. 26. Glue and nail G to A,B,C,D,E and with 4 penny finishing nails spaced 10 to 12" apart, Illus. 19.

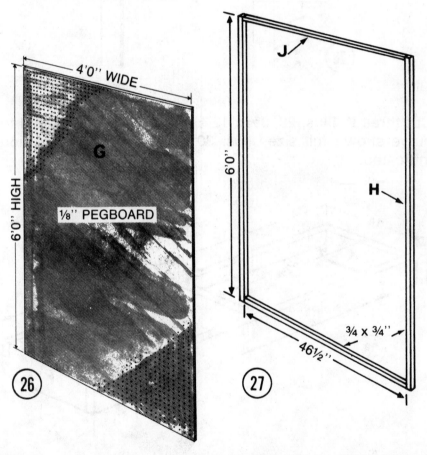

Saw 1 x 2 in half. Cut two H, two J, Illus. 27, to size indicated. Glue and nail HJ to back of assembled unit, Illus. 28. HJ spaces back unit ¾" from wall. This permits using pegboard tool holders in G.

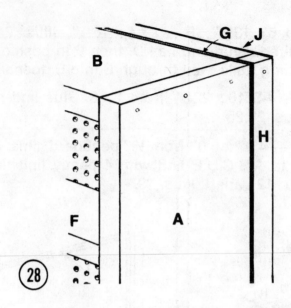

Cut three K, Illus. 29, 3⅜ x 12⅞" from 5/4 x 4". Cut end to curve shown full size, Illus. 30. Drill ½" hole in position indicated.

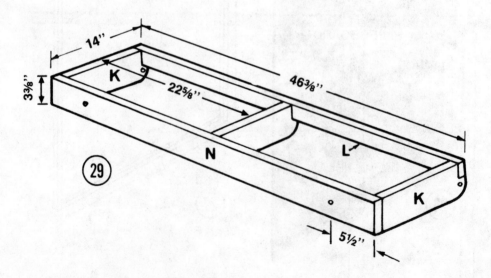

Cut N — 3⅜ x 46⅜".

Cut L 5/4 x 1½ x 46⅜". Apply glue and assemble KLN with 8 penny finishing nails, Illus. 29.

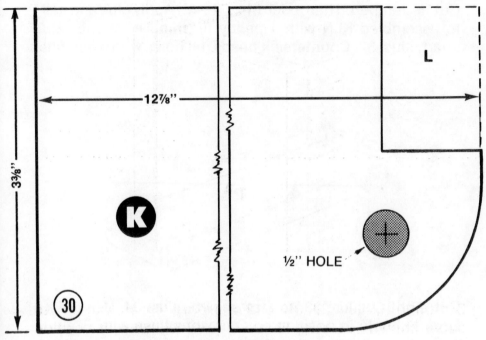

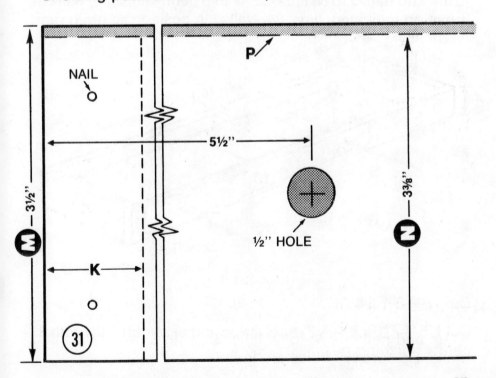

Showing position of hole in M,N.

Cut ⅛" tempered hardboard 14 x 46⅜". Apply glue and nail P to assembled KLN with 4 penny finishing nails spaced 6" apart, Illus. 32. Countersink heads, fill holes with wood filler.

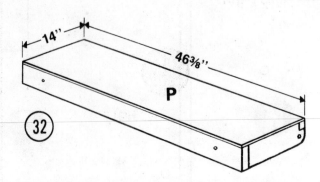

Cut eight Q, Illus. 33, to size shown, Illus. 34. Use 5/4 x 4. Bore ½" hole in position so Q finishes flush with P.

Glue and nail Q to N, Illus. 33, with 6 penny finishing nails in position indicated, Illus. 34. Nail Q in position so grain runs vertically.

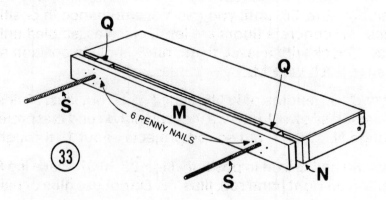

Glue and nail one M to Q, Illus. 33, with 6 penny finishing nails. Be sure ½" holes are in line.

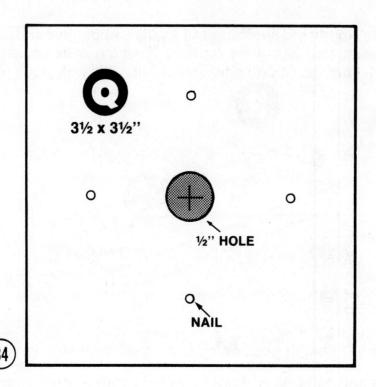

Q

3½ x 3½"

½" HOLE

NAIL

(34)

Cut two legs R, 34" or length required for adult bench; 26 to 30" for child size, Illus. 35. Use 5/4 x 4. Do not drill ½" hole in position, Illus. 36, until you can test workbench in position. Since few concrete floors are level, place assembled unit in place. Check with a level, then drill ½" hole in position so R finishes flush with M.

Cut two 18" lengths of ½" threaded steel rod, Illus. 33. Insert in position shown. Place washer and nut on end that projects through N. Tighten nut so rod projects about 1" through N.

Glue and nail Q to M in position, Illus. 33,36,37. Place leg R in position on right hand rod, Illus. 36. Do not use glue or nail as leg must swing freely on rod.

Glue and nail Q to M on left hand rod, Illus. 36. Place M in position. Glue and nail M to Q. Place leg R on left hand rod. Glue and nail Q to M on right hand rod. Place M in position. Glue and nail M to Q.

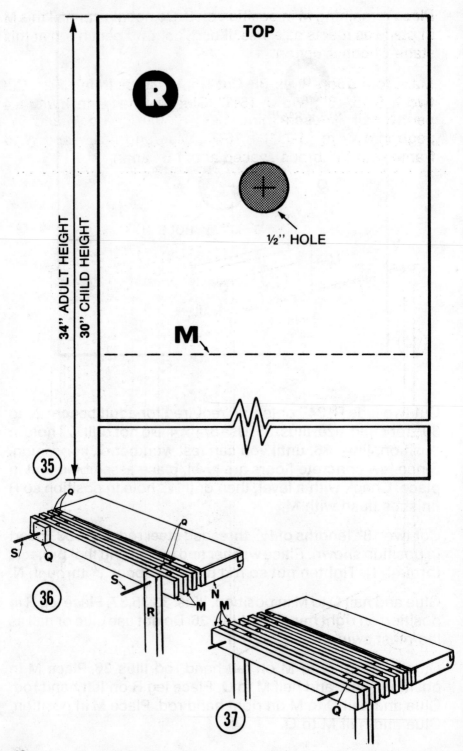

TOP

R

½" HOLE

34" ADULT HEIGHT

30" CHILD HEIGHT

M

35

Q

Q

S

Q

S

R

M

N

36

M

M

Q

37

Place remaining M in position on S. Do not glue or nail this M in place as it acts as a vise. Illus. 37 shows bench top at this stage of construction.

Make four doors, Illus. 38. Cut ¾ x ¾" strips from 1 x 2". Cut two T, 9-15/16"; two U, 16¾". Glue and nail U to T with a 4 penny nail at each joint. Cut ⅛" hardboard V and ⅛" pegboard W to 11-7/16 x 16¾". Glue and nail V and W to frame with ¾" brads spaced about 6" apart.

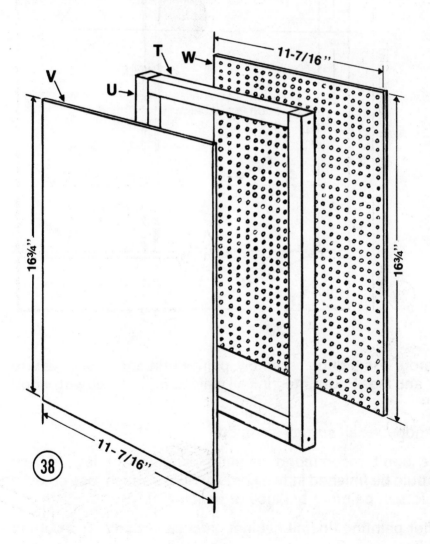

38

Mortise edge of door to receive full thickness of a closed 2 x 2" hinge. Bore hole to receive screw for door pull. Hang doors, Illus. 19, with 2 x 2" loose pin butt hinges. If necessary, plane or sandpaper doors to fit. Fasten 1" door pulls in position indicated, Illus. 39.

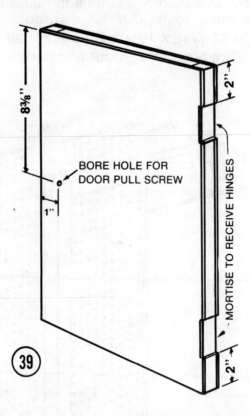

BORE HOLE FOR DOOR PULL SCREW

MORTISE TO RECEIVE HINGES

Before completing assembly, paint workbench. Remove vise M, and legs R. Countersink all nailheads, fill holes with wood filler.

Sandpaper all surfaces smooth.

We don't recommend painting benchtop or legs. These should be finished in two coats of Spar Varnish. Use colorful colors in painting balance of bench.

After painting, install cabinet catches to doors and bottom of F.

Make two vise handles, Illus. 40. Cut 1" aluminum tubing X, 8", Illus. 41. Bore 9/16" clear through where indicated. Bore 1/32" holes where indicated. Cut ⅞" dowel Y, 8¾", Illus. 42. Round ends with file and sandpaper. Bore 9/16" hole through center. Saw Y in half. Notch each to receive nut Z, Illus. 40.

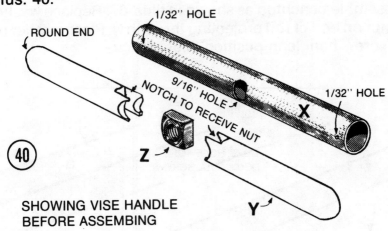

1/32" HOLE

ROUND END

9/16" HOLE

NOTCH TO RECEIVE NUT

1/32" HOLE

X

Z

Y

(40)

SHOWING VISE HANDLE
BEFORE ASSEMBING

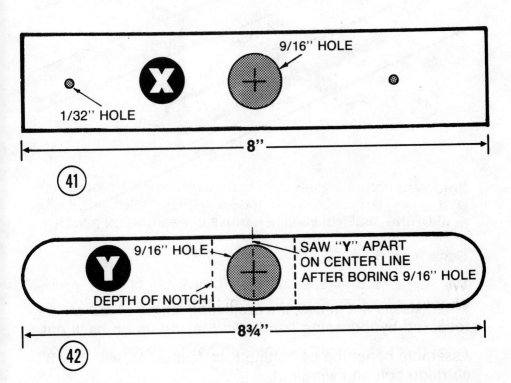

9/16" HOLE

X

1/32" HOLE

|← 8" →|

(41)

Y

9/16" HOLE

SAW "Y" APART
ON CENTER LINE
AFTER BORING 9/16" HOLE

DEPTH OF NOTCH

|← 8¾" →|

(42)

43

Assemble handle, Illus. 43. Drive half of Y into X so 9/16'' hole lines up. Place nut Z in position. Drive other half of Y in position. Screw Z onto S to make certain it's locked in position. Remove and secure Y in position by driving ¾'' wire nails through holes in X.

Reassemble benchtop as shown in Illus. 37. Replace washer and nut on end of rod projecting through N. Place washer on rod, screw handle in position, Illus. 43.

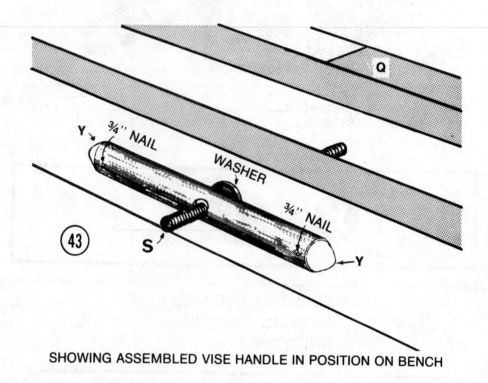

SHOWING ASSEMBLED VISE HANDLE IN POSITION ON BENCH

When vise is not in use, the projecting length of rod can be recessed by loosening handle and taking up on back nut.

Assemble benchtop by bolting K to A, Illus. 44, with ½ x 3'' carriage bolt and wing nut.

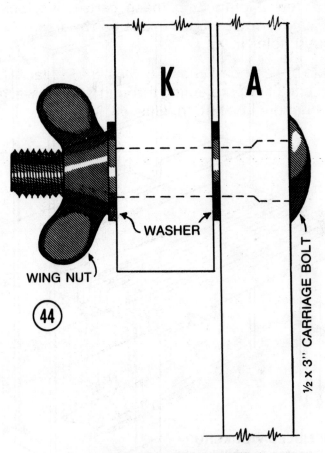

K

A

WASHER

WING NUT

(44)

½ x 3" CARRIAGE BOLT

FULL SIZE END VIEW
SHOWING BENCH-TOP
BOLTED IN POSITION

Place assembled unit in position where legs on bench stand level. Fasten A to wall with 2 x 2'' angle irons, Illus. 45.

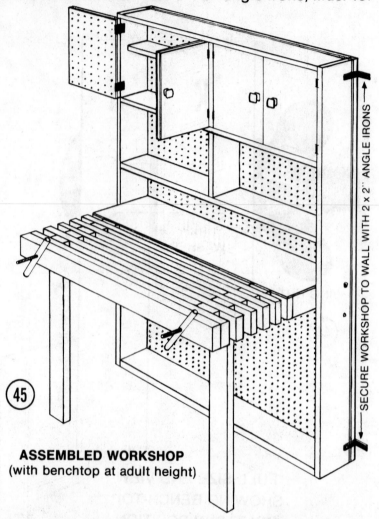

ASSEMBLED WORKSHOP
(with benchtop at adult height)

NOTE: Best working height naturally varies with height of person using bench. We located benchtop at a comfortable average working height. If you are exceptionally tall or short, raise or lower benchtop. Before boring ½'' hole through A or cutting R to length, determine height suited to your requirements. Cut legs and bore ½'' holes through A where required.

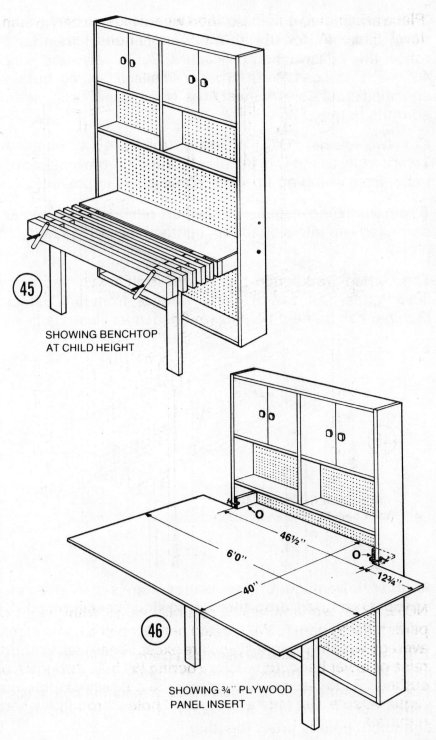

(45)

SHOWING BENCHTOP
AT CHILD HEIGHT

46½"

6'0"

40"

12¾"

(46)

SHOWING ¾" PLYWOOD
PANEL INSERT

This workshop can be used in many ways. To insert a large panel, Illus. 46, for use as a sewing center or train table, follow this construction procedure. Cut ¾" plywood panel 40" x 6'. Panel can be cut larger or smaller if desired, but size specified is suitable for most uses. Notch panel as illustrated so it fits between A.

Cut two cleats "O" 5½" long from 5/4 x 4, Illus. 46. Temporarily clamp O in position. Cleats "O" prevent back of panel from swinging up when panel is slid in position.

To put workshop in foldaway position, remove O, loosen vise, swing legs up into slotted top, tighten vise, swing benchtop down.

The slotted workbench top shown in Illus. 47, has many advantages. Cut two 6" long wedges from 5/4" stock. Material can be held tight in workbench as illustrated.

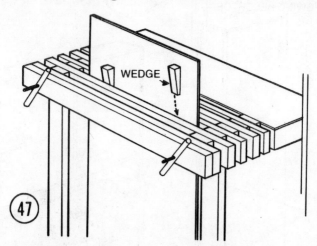

WEDGE

47

Another advantage of the slotted top is the shavings, sawdust, etc., will drop through to floor keeping working surface clear.

The benchtop can also be used as a clamp for gluing boards, Illus. 48. Bore ⅜" holes 2" deep in top edge of vise M. Drop ⅜ x 2" machine bolts in holes. Head of machine bolt acts as bench "dog." Wedges hold edge of board. When vise is tightened, boards press together.

48

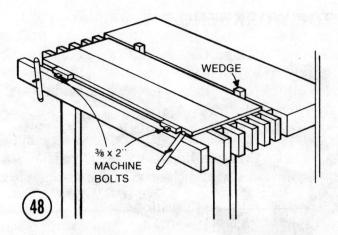

WEDGE

³⁄₈ x 2''
MACHINE
BOLTS

(48)

If you wish to use as a gardening center, Illus. 49, assemble framing to size noted. Fasten to A with four ³⁄₈ x 2" carriage bolts and washers.

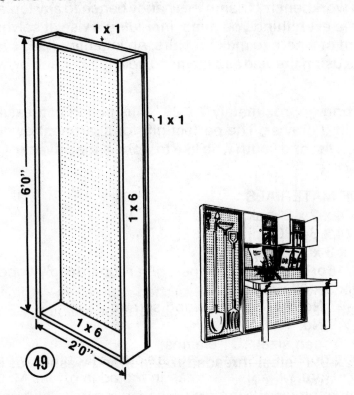

1 x 1

1 x 1

6'0"

1 x 6

1 x 6

2'0"

(49)

Countersink all screws. Fill holes with wood filler. To make an excellent filler, mix sawdust with glue.

TABLE TOP WORKBENCH

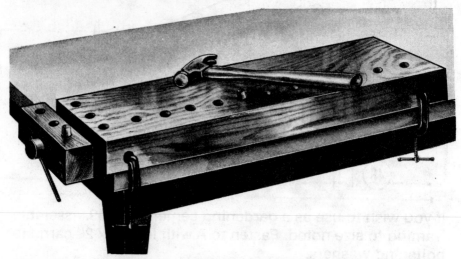

Need a workbench? Clamp this handy bench to any table and you have everything you need, including a vise. It solves the problem of where to make repairs. An ingenious peg system permits using the vise as a clamp to hold lumber and plywood up to 2' wide.

Measuring approximately 7 x 28", this bench can easily be stored in a drawer. The perfect gift for apartment dwellers, the hobbyist and youth who like to work in the privacy of their own room.

LIST OF MATERIALS
    1 — 5/4 x 2 x 2' oak, A,B,L
    1 — 5/4 x 6 x 30" pine, C
    1 — 1 x 3 x 5' pine, D
    1 — 3/16 or ¼ x 8 x 30" tempered hardboard or plywood,E,F
    1 — 2 x 3 x 8" oak, G
    6 — 1¾" No. 10 flathead wood screws
  12 — 1¼" No. 10   ''   ''   ''
    2 — 2" (open size) "C" clamps
    1 — ½ x 9⅛" steel threaded rod, nut and washer for K
  4" — ¾" dowel for N
  ½ x 17" steel rod for H, unthreaded
  ¼ x 6" steel rod for M
    1 box ¾" brads

Cut two A — 5/4 x 1½ x 5½", Illus. 50. Bore 3/16" holes through A where indicated.

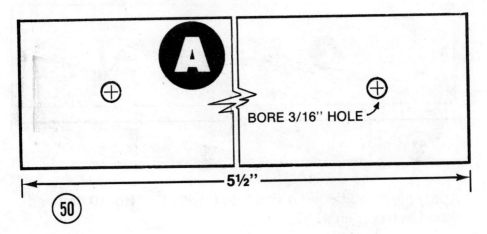

BORE 3/16" HOLE

5½"

50

Cut nut block B same size, Illus. 51. Bore 3/16" holes through B where indicated. Mortise shaded area 1" deep to overall size a ½" nut for a threaded bolt requires. To mortise, first bore ⅜" holes 1" deep in position indicated, then cut holes square using a ¼ or ⅜" chisel. Insert nut in cutout.

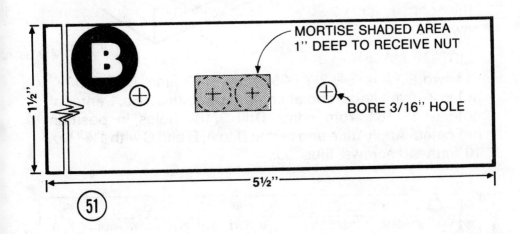

MORTISE SHADED AREA
1" DEEP TO RECEIVE NUT

BORE 3/16" HOLE

1½"

5½"

51

Cut C, Illus. 52. to size indicated from 5/4 x 6" pine.

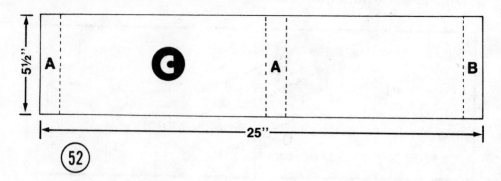

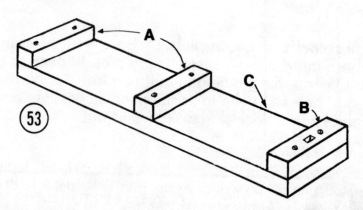

Apply glue and fasten A and B to C with 1¾" No. 10 flathead wood screws, Illus. 53.

Cut two D, Illus. 54, 2¼ x 25" from 1 x 3 pine. Drill two ¾" holes 2" from ends, and at angle shown, Illus. 55a. Center of hole is 11/16" from edge. Drill 3/16" holes in position indicated. Apply glue and fasten D to A, B and C with 1¼" No. 10 flathead screws, Illus. 55.

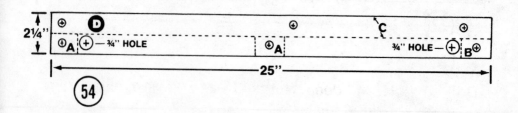

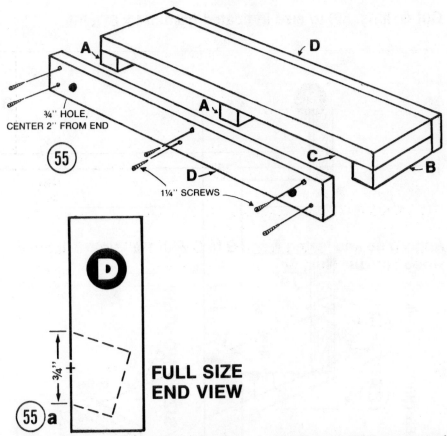

A

D

¾" HOLE,
CENTER 2" FROM END

A

C

B

(55)

1¼" SCREWS

D

D

FULL SIZE
END VIEW

¾"

(55)a

Cut benchtop E to size shown, Illus. 56, from 3/16" tempered hardboard or ¼" plywood. Apply glue and nail E to C and D with ¾" brads. Apply weight to bond E in place.

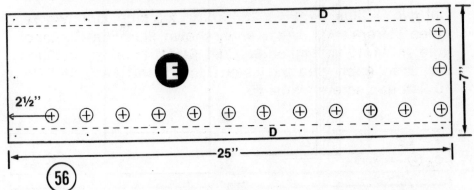

D

E

7"

2½"

25"

D

(56)

Drill ¾" holes, 1" deep. Note full size end view, Illus. 57, in position shown in Illus. 58.

53

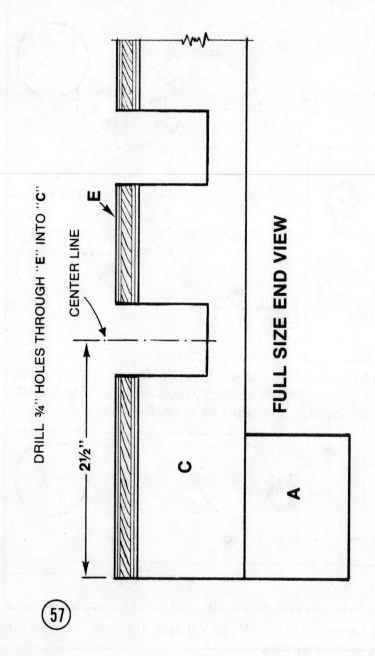

DRILL ¾" HOLES THROUGH "E" INTO "C"

CENTER LINE

E

2½"

C

A

FULL SIZE END VIEW

(57)

54

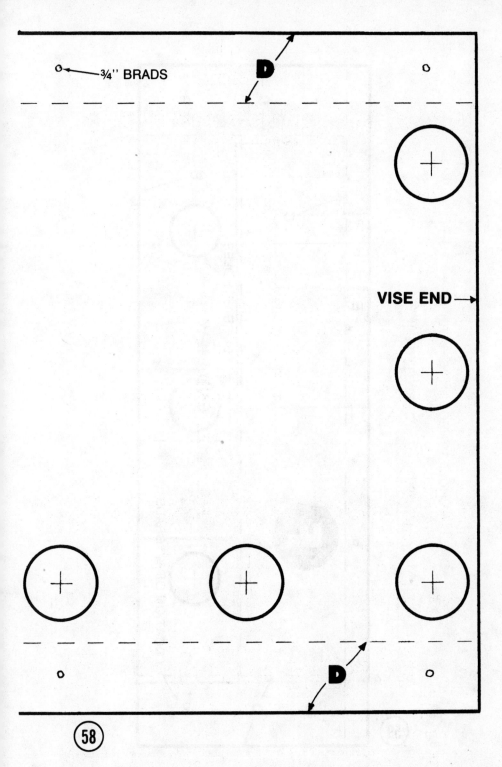

¾'' BRADS

D

VISE END →

D

58

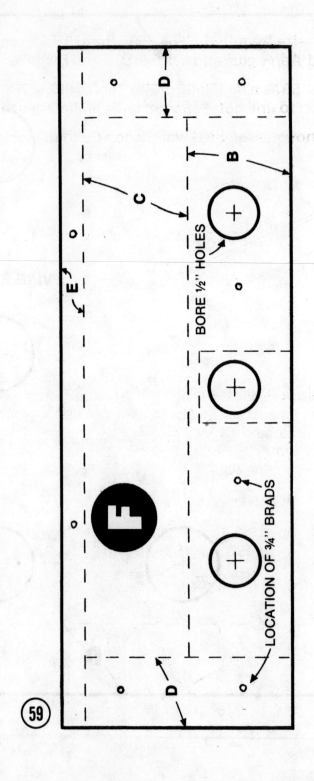

BORE ½" HOLES

LOCATION OF ¾" BRADS

B

C

D

D

E

F

59

56

Cut F to size required, Illus. 59, from 3/16" tempered hardboard. Apply glue and nail F to B, D and E with ¾" brads.

Using Illus. 59 as a template, drill ½" holes through F and B. Use caution to drill holes straight and parallel to each other.

Illus. 60 shows assembled workbench up to this point.

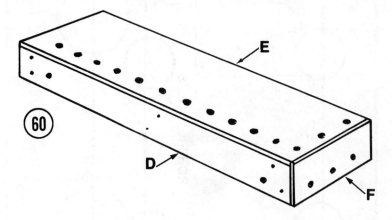

Cut vise block G, Illus. 61, 2½ x 7" from oak, maple or other hardwood, Illus. 61,62. Illus. 62 is a full size pattern. Fold along line indicated. Drill ¾" holes, 1" deep; two ½" holes, 1" deep. Drill center ½" hole through G. Holes must be level, parallel and in line with those drilled in F, Illus. 60.

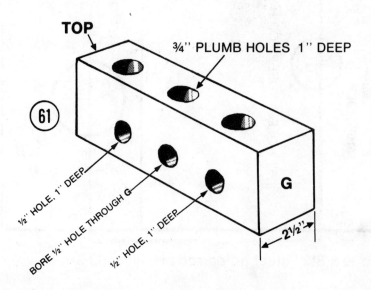

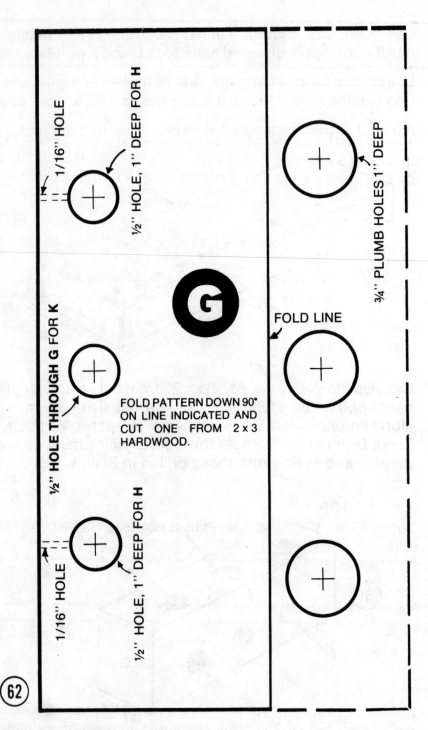

1/16" HOLE

1/2" HOLE, 1" DEEP FOR H

1/2" HOLE THROUGH G FOR K

FOLD PATTERN DOWN 90°
ON LINE INDICATED AND
CUT ONE FROM 2 x 3
HARDWOOD.

1/16" HOLE

1/2" HOLE, 1" DEEP FOR H

G

FOLD LINE

3/4" PLUMB HOLES 1" DEEP

62

Cut two 1/2 x 8¼" steel guide rods H, Illus. 63,64.

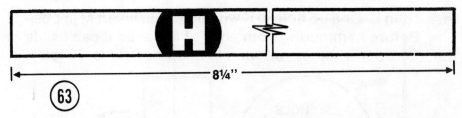

8¼"

(63)

Drive H into G in position shown, Illus. 64. Turn G bottom face up. Using a steel bit, drill a 1/16" hole through G and H, Illus. 62. Drive a 3 penny nail through H to lock H in position.

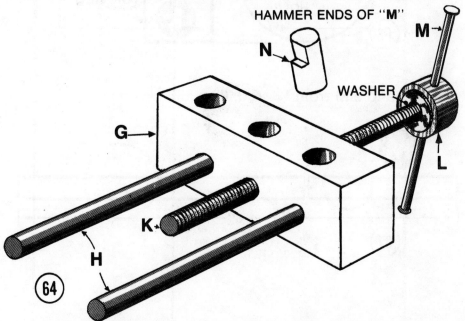

HAMMER ENDS OF "M"

M→

N→

WASHER

G→

K→

L

H

(64)

Cut ½ x 9½" threaded steel rod K, Illus. 64,65. Drill ¼" hole 5/16" from end.

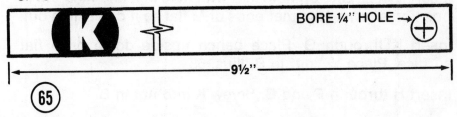

K

BORE ¼" HOLE →

9½"

(65)

Cut hub L, Illus. 66, ¾" from 5/4 x 2 oak. Drill a ½" hole, ⅝" deep in center. Drill ¼" hole through L in position indicated.

Insert K in L. Line up hole in K with hole in L. Insert M in position. Before hammering both ends of M flat so it can't slide out, consider whether you want to add vise P, Illus. 70 to 74.

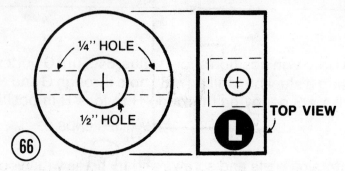

¼" HOLE

½" HOLE

TOP VIEW

66

L

Cut 6" handle M from ¼" rod, Illus. 67.

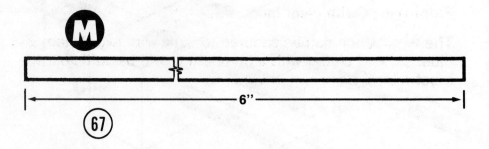

M

|—————————— 6" ——————————|

67

Place ½" diameter washer on K, Illus. 64.

Insert K in L. Line up hole in K with hole in L and insert M in position shown. Hammer ends of M flat so it can't slide out.

Insert K through G. Place bench upside down on a flat surface. Place ½" nut in B, Illus. 53.

Insert H through F and B. Screw K into nut in B.

Cut two 1½" lengths of ¾" dowel, Illus. 68, for pegs N. If necessary, sandpaper N so it fits easily into ¾" holes in E and G. If you file one edge flat, Illus. 68, it provides a better face when butting against board.

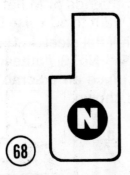

Countersink nails and screws and fill holes with wood filler. Sandpaper all surfaces smooth.

Glue strips of ¼" foam rubber to A and B.

Paint bench with clear lacquer.

The workbench can be secured to table with two C clamps, Illus. 69, A C clamp with a 3" opening will be sufficient for most tables.

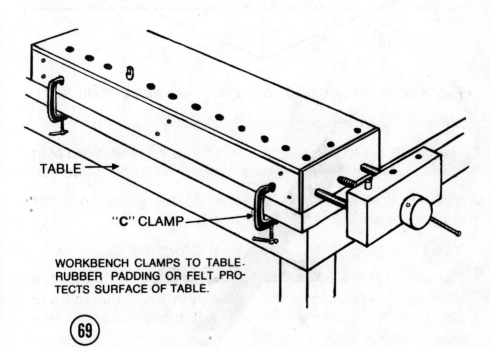

TABLE →

"C" CLAMP

WORKBENCH CLAMPS TO TABLE. RUBBER PADDING OR FELT PRO-TECTS SURFACE OF TABLE.

(69)

A self opening vise can be made by following optional construction shown in Illus. 70 to 74.

Cut two pieces of 1/16" thick flat steel — 1¼ x 1¼" for plate P. Bore and countersink ⅝" No. 3 flathead wood screws, Illus. 70. Screw pieces in place on a scrap piece of wood. Bore ⅜" hole in center as shown.

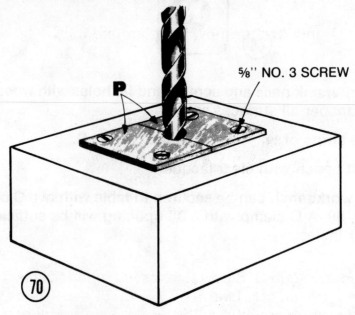

⅝" NO. 3 SCREW

P

70

File a ⅛" wide slot 1/16" deep, ¾" from end of K, Illus. 71.

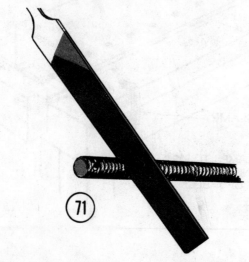

71

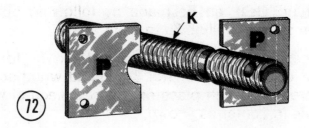

(72)

Illus. 72 and 73 show how P fits around K.

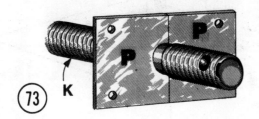

(73) K

Slide K through G. Screw P in place around K, Illus. 74. Slip hub L over end of K. Line up ¼" holes in L and K. Slide handle M in position through L and K. Hammer both ends of M flat so that M cannot slide out of assembled LK.

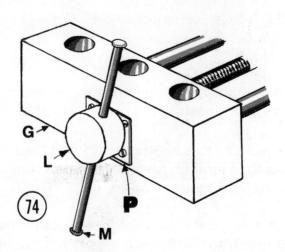

(74)

SAWHORSE TOOL CHEST

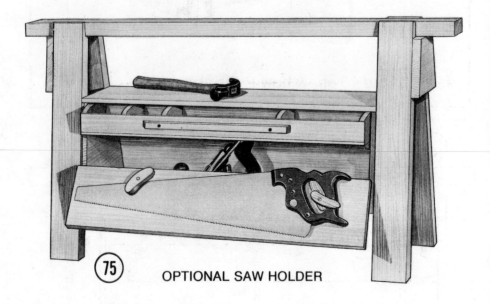

(75)   OPTIONAL SAW HOLDER

LIST OF MATERIALS
  1 — 2 x 4 x 14', A,B
  1 — ½" x 4 x 4' plywood, C,D,E,F,G,H,J,K,L,M,N,O,R
  3 — 1" No. 8 flathead wood screws
 12 — ¾" No. 6   "   "   "
  2 — 1¼" No. 8   "   "   "
¼" plywood scraps, Q
¼ lb. each 4, 6 and 10 penny finishing nails
1 pair butterfly hinges

Due to the variance in lumber width and thickness, always cut notches to fit lumber. Always cut inner framing members to size assembly requires.

Cut one rail A — 2 x 4 x 47". Notch A in position shown, Illus. 76,77. Cut notch to width 2 x 4 legs B require, Illus. 78.

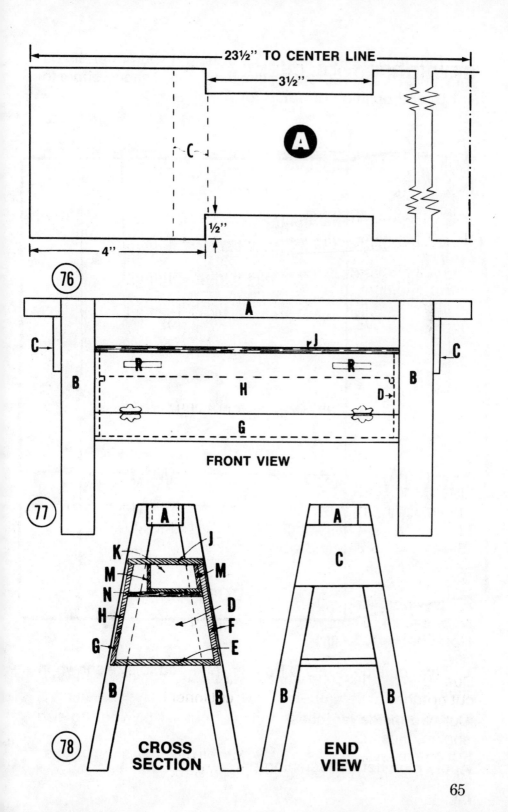

23½" TO CENTER LINE

3½"

C

A

½"

4"

76

A

C

J

R

R

C

B

H

D

B

G

FRONT VIEW

77

A

K

J

M

M

N

H

D

G

F

E

B

B

78

CROSS
SECTION

A

C

B

B

END
VIEW

Cut four legs B — 2 x 4 x 24¼", or height you prefer. If you fold Illus. 79,80 — 90° along line indicated, it shows angle to cut B, and position of notch for A.

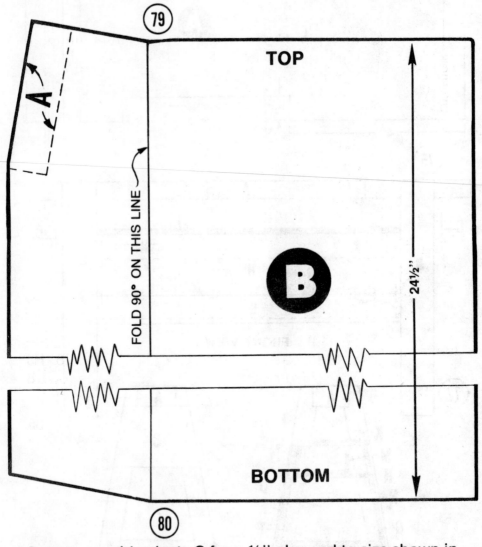

Cut two outside cleats C from ½" plywood to size shown in Illus. 81.

Cut two inside leg chest ends D from ½" plywood to size shown, Illus. 82.

Apply glue before fastening parts.

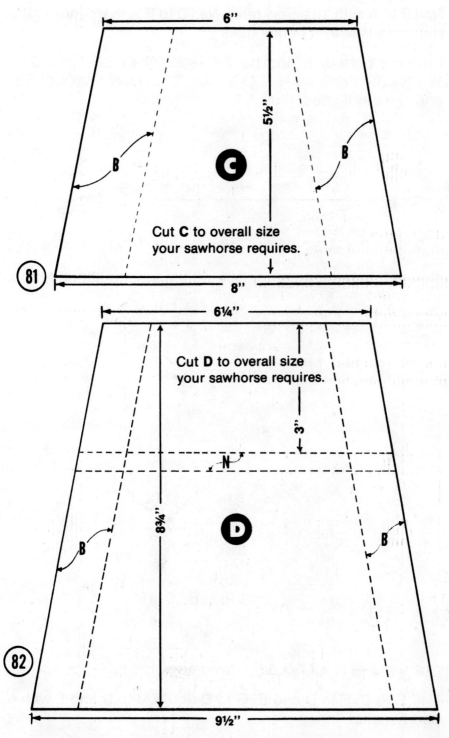

6"

5½"

B

C

B

Cut **C** to overall size
your sawhorse requires.

⑧⑴

8"

6¼"

Cut **D** to overall size
your sawhorse requires.

3"

N

8¾"

B

D

B

⑧⒉

9½"

Nail B to A with 10 penny nails. Nail D to B with 6 penny nails. Nail C to B with 8 penny nails.

Cut one bottom E and back F — ½ x 9⅝ x 32"; one G — ½ x 3 x 32"; one lid H — ½ x 6¾ x 32". Bevel edges of E,F and H as indicated, Illus. 83.

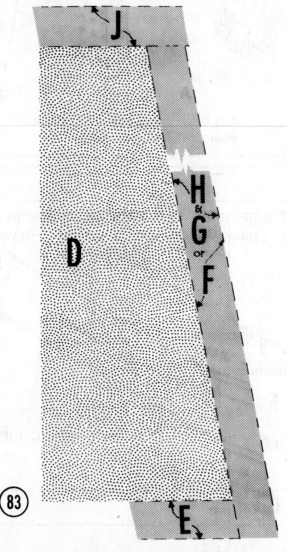

83

Cut top J — ½ x 7¼ x 32". Bevel edges.

Nail E to D, F to D and E, G to D and E, J to D and F with 6 penny nails.

Cut five K from ½'' plywood to size shown, Illus. 84.

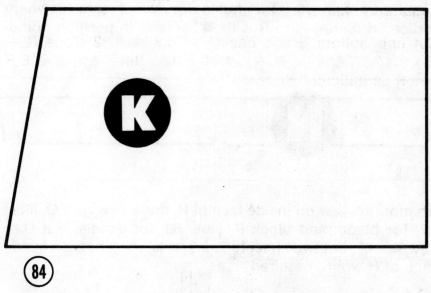

(84)

Cut one tray bottom L — ½ x 5⅜ x 30¾''; one front M — ½ x 2½ x 30¾''; one back M — ½ x 2⅝ x 30¾''. Bevel edges, Illus. 85.

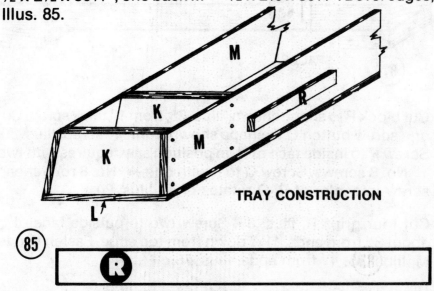

TRAY CONSTRUCTION

(85)

Nail front and back M to end K.

Nail L to K and M with 4 penny nails. Space other partitions K to suit your needs.

Cut two tray slides N — ½ x ½ x 7½". Bevel ends to shape required, Illus. 86. Drill holes for No. 6 screws where indicated. Screw N to D with ¾" screws in position noted, Illus. 82.

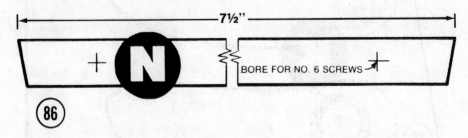

|←————————————— 7½" —————————————→|

BORE FOR NO. 6 SCREWS

86

To mount a saw on inside face of H, make saw rack O, Illus. 87, for blade; and block P, Illus. 88, for handle. Cut O — ½ x ¾ x 6"; cut two spacers ¼ x ¾ x ¾". Mount O on inside face of H where required.

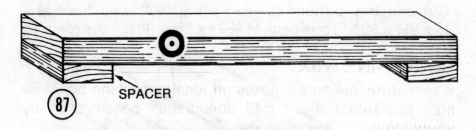

SPACER

87

Cut block P to shape shown, Illus. 88, from 1" thick scrap. Cut one screw button Q to shape shown from ¼" scrap, Illus. 89. Screw P to inside face of H, in position saw requires with two 1" No. 8 screws. Screw Q to P with one ¾" No. 8 roundhead screw in center of P. Q rotates on P, Illus. 90.

Cut four grips R, Illus. 85. Screw two to outside face of H about 3" from ends, 1¼" down from top edge. Fasten two to M, Illus. 85, 4" from ends, Illus. 75.

Hinge H to G with two butterfly hinges, Illus. 77.

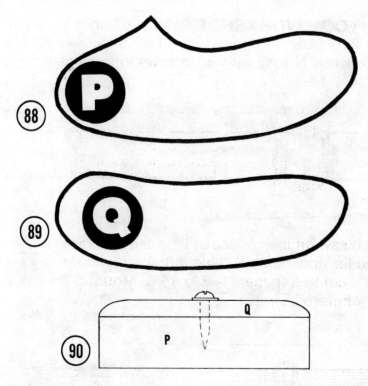

SHOESHINE BOX

A miniature sawhorse makes an ideal shoeshine box. Full size Easi-Bild Pattern #45 encourages construction by youngsters.

71

POWER TOOL WORKSHOP

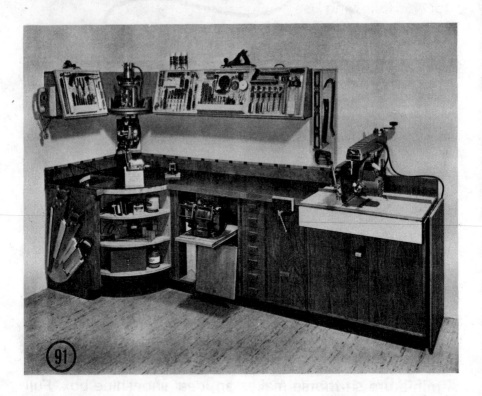

While directions simplify building each cabinet to a specific size, each can be built to fit space available. A countertop can be cut to cover each counter or those along one wall.

The first step is to measure space available and to rough in wiring. Book #694 Electrical Repairs Simplified explains how to install needed base outlets and lighting.

Select and build cabinets to provide the work area and storage space required for use with the tool recommended.

To fill space available, cut back, bottom, shelves, spreader and countertop to length required. Always maintain the 22¼'' front-to-back dimension. The easiest way to measure exact length is to cut ends. Place in position and measure length required for shelves, back, etc.

The numbered cabinets shown in Illus. 92 are recommended for the following use:

1 — GRINDER AND STORAGE DRAWER CABINET
Storage galore, plus a pullout sliding shelf that permits easy access to grinder.

2 — SAW HORSE CABINET
Convenient storage for collapsible saw horse.

3 — TOTE BOX AND STORAGE DRAWER CABINET
A carpenter-styled tote box accommodates wall tool panel, stores away when not in use.

4 — CORNER WORK BENCH
Contains a 4 tiered circular lazy-susan that utilizes all corner space.

5 — RADIAL ARM SAW BENCH
Heavy duty workbench with sliding drop leaf extension table. Mounted on casters. Lever permits moving bench where job requires.

6 — WALL CABINET WITH REVOLVING TOOL TURRET
Accommodates tools in a handy space saving arrangement.

7 — WALL STORAGE UNIT
Provides convenient surface storage for sander, drill, circular saw, jig saw and other tools.

8 — ROLLING LUMBER RACK
Takes needed material to the job in this easy-to-move storage rack.

(92)

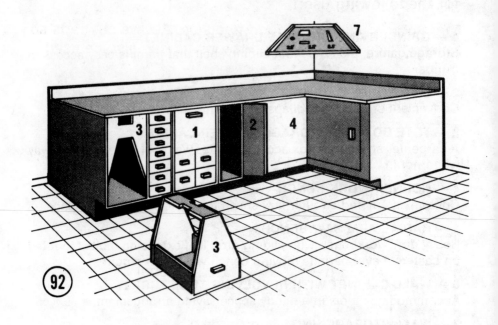

We suggest using ⅝ or ¾'' plywood or flakeboard for all parts except where other material is specified.

GRINDER AND STORAGE DRAWER CABINET

LIST OF MATERIAL

Buy ⅝ or ¾'' plywood, good one side. Always cut parts so finished face is on outside. Flakeboard can also be used.

2 — **A** - End - ¾ x 22¼ x 32¼''
1 — **B** - Back - ¾ x 14 x 28¾''
2 — **C** - Bottom Shelf - ¾ x 14 x 21½''
1 — **D** - Grinder Platform - ¾ x 14 x 20½''
2 — **E** - Top - ¾ x 15 x 23'''*
1 — **F** - Divider - ¾ x 12¾ x 21½''
1 — **G** - Door - ¾ x 14 x 14½''
1 — **H** - Spacer - ¾ x 5¾ x 14''
2 — **K** - Cleat - ¾ x 3½ x 18½''
1 — **L** - Toe Board - ¾ x 3½ x 15½'' optional
1 — **M** - Splashboard - ¾ x 5½ x 15½''
4 — **N** - Drawer Front - ¾ x 6⅜ x 6⅝''
4 — **O** - Drawer Back - ¾ x 6⅛ x 6⅛''
8 — **P** - Drawer Side - ¾ x 6⅜ x 21¼'' use 1 x 8
4 — **Q** - Drawer Bottom - ¼ x 6⅜ x 21¼'' hardboard**
1 — **R** - Tray Front - ¾ x 3½ x 14''
1 — **S** - Tray Back - ¾ x 3½ x 13½''
2 — **T** - Tray Side - ¾ x 3½ x 20¼''
1 — **U** - Tray Bottom - ¼ x 14 x 20½'' hardboard**
8 — **V** - Drawer Slide - ¼ x ¾ x 20¾'' hardwood
2 — **W** - Tray Slide - ⅛ x ¾ x 20½'' hardwood
4 — **X** - Drawer Pull - 1 x 3
1 — friction catch, 1 pr. fast pin cabinet door hinges for ¾'' flush door, plus 1 drawer track will be needed. Use ⅛ or ¼'' hardboard to cover top, front and exposed ends.

*Use single or double thickness plywood for top. Cut shelf to width grinder requires.
**⅛'' hardboard or ¼'' plywood can be used for drawer and tray bottoms.

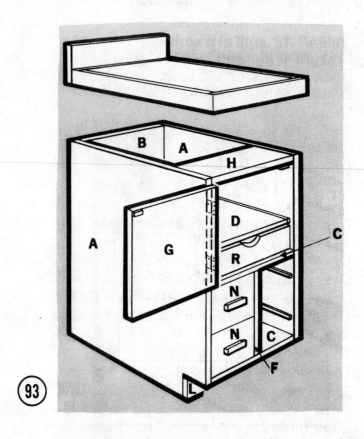

The cutting chart, Illus. 94, shows an economical layout to cut parts from ⅝ or ¾'' plywood. Always measure space available for inner parts, then cut each when directions require same. Cabinet shown, Illus. 93, consists of two ends A, one back B, two C, one H, one F, four drawers, one door G. Base L can be cut to fit cabinet or cut to length required for all cabinets along one wall.

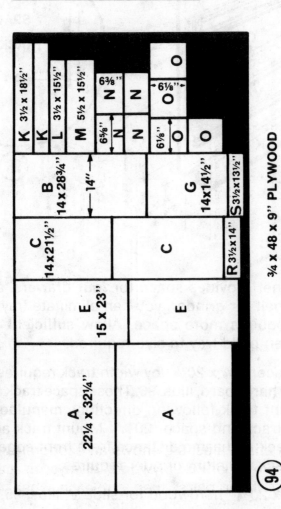

CUTTING DIAGRAM

D 14"

H 5¾ x 14"

F 12¾"

K 3½ x 18½"

K

L 3½ x 15½"

M 5½ x 15½"

N 6⅜"

N 6⅝"

N

N

O

O 6⅛"

O 6⅛"

O

B 14 x 28¾"

14"

C 14 x 21½"

C

G 14 x 14½"

S 3½ x 13½"

R 3½ x 14"

E 15 x 23"

E

A 22¼ x 32¼"

A

94

¾ x 48 x 9" PLYWOOD
Use 1 x 4 x 4' for T

Notch front end of A — 3½ x 3¾'', Illus. 95. Cut two K and other parts to size indicated or required.

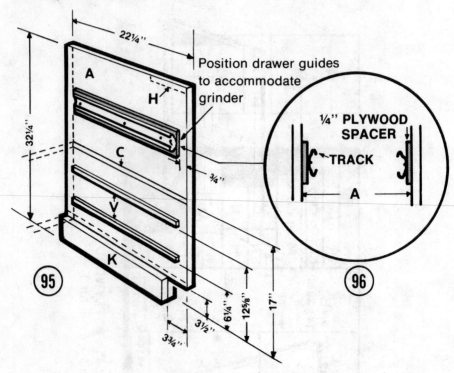

While cabinet provides space for four drawers, a tray and slide out shelf for grinder, you can eliminate tray if grinder selected requires more space. Allow sufficient space for grinder, then build tray to size required.

Cut two spacers, ¼ x 20¾'' by width track requires, from ¼'' plywood or hardboard, Illus. 96. These space track away from sides. Mount track following directions manufacturer provides. Cut track and spacer 20¾''. Mount track and spacer ¾'' from back and same distance from front edge, Illus. 95. Position track at height grinder requires.

Cut ¼ x ¾ x 20¾'' hardwood for slide V, Illus. 95. Glue and brad in position.

Glue and nail A to C; A to B; B to C; C and B to F; A to H, Illus. 93, 95, 97, 98. Countersink heads, fill holes with wood filler.

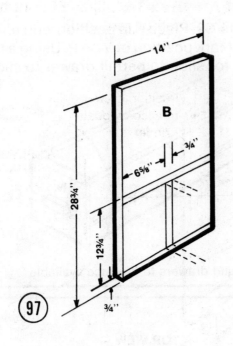

(97)

14"

B

3/4"

6 5/8"

28 3/4"

12 3/4"

3/4"

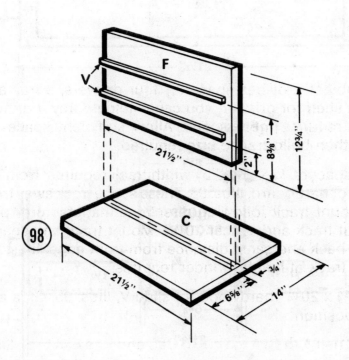

(98)

F

V

21 1/2"

8 3/8"

12 3/4"

2"

C

21 1/2"

6 5/8"

3/4"

14"

79

DRAWERS

Cut two sides P, Illus. 99. Place P in position with end butting against V, Illus. 95. Mark position of V on P. Using a table saw or router, rout slot for slide to permit drawer to slide freely.

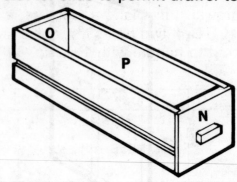

Build drawers to fit space available

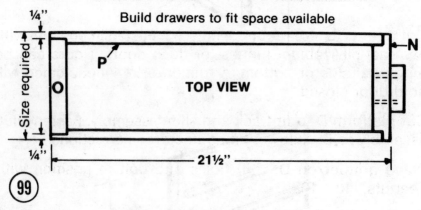

TOP VIEW

¼"

Size required

¼"

21½"

(99)

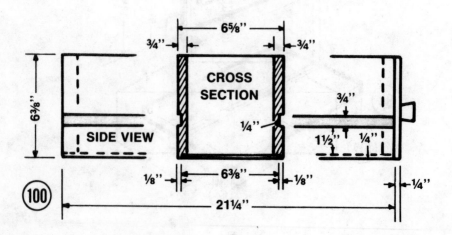

CROSS SECTION

SIDE VIEW

6⅝"

¾" — ¾"

6⅜"

⅛" — 6⅜" — ⅛"

21¼"

6⅜"

¾"

1½" ¼"

¼"

(100)

As Illus. 100 indicates, slot runs to within ¼" of front. This acts as a stop. After rabbeting, glue and nail sides to back and front. Glue and nail ¼" hardboard bottom in position shown, Illus. 100.

To make a drawer pull, plane a piece of ¾ x ¾ x 3" to ⅛" bevel, Illus. 101. Drill two holes through drawer front, Illus. 99. Fasten front to handle with 1¼" No. 8 flathead screws.

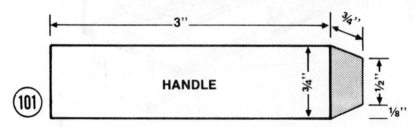

Cut door G to size required, Illus. 93. Fasten in position with two fast-pin cabinet hinges for flush doors. Doors can be hinged at side or bottom. A friction or magnetic catch will hold door closed.

Cut platform D to fit track and slide assembly. Fasten slide assembly to D, following manufacturer's directions.

Place grinder on D. Drill holes and bolt in position with Teenuts, Illus. 102.

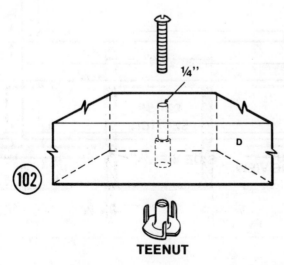

TEENUT

TRAY

Cut sides T, back S and front R to height space permits, Illus. 103. Shape front as shown.

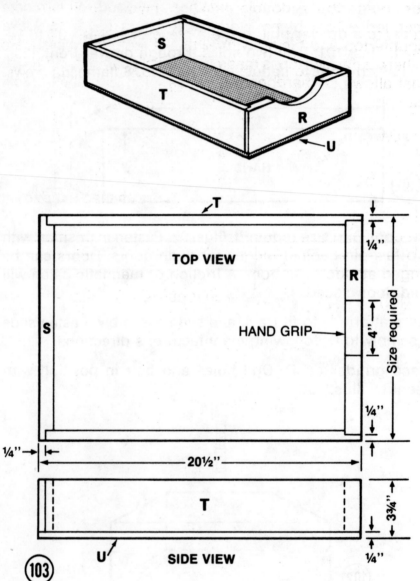

TOP VIEW

¼"

R

HAND GRIP

4"

Size required

S

¼"

¼"

20½"

T

3¾"

¼"

U

SIDE VIEW

(103)

COUNTER TOP — BACK SPLASHER

Cut back splasher 5½" by length required, Illus. 104. Apply glue and nail back splasher to a ¾ x 23" by length required for countertop. A double thickness plywood top is recommended where heavy work is going to be done. Cover countertop and facing with ⅛ or ¼" tempered hardboard. Where a countertop is made for a single cabinet, cut to size that allows ⅛" hardboard to finish flush with ends on end cabinet.

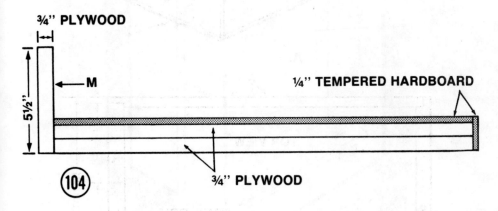

¾" PLYWOOD

5½"

← M

¼" TEMPERED HARDBOARD

104

¾" PLYWOOD

SAWHORSE STORAGE CABINET

The cabinet shown, Illus. 105, should be constructed to width required to accommodate come-a-part sawhorse legs. The 7" width for bottom C is minimal.

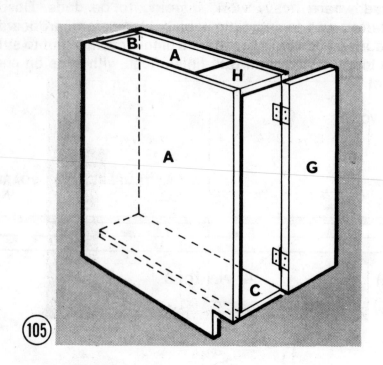

(105)

LIST OF MATERIAL

2 — **A** - End - ¾ x 22¼ x 32¼"
1 — **B** - Back - ¾ x 7 x 28¾"
1 — **C** - Bottom - ¾ x 7 x 21½"
2 — **D** - Top - ¾ x 8 x 23" optional
1 — **F** - Back Splash - ¾ x 5¾ x 8½" optional
1 — **G** - Door - ¾ x 7 x 27¼"
1 — **H** - Spacer - ¾ x 5¾ x 7"
2 — **K** - Base - ¾ x 3½ x 18½"
1 — **L** - Toeboard - ¾ x 3½ x length required - optional
1 pr. cabinet hinges
1 magnetic catch

Revise cutting chart, Illus. 106, to accommodate any changes you make in overall size. Cut two A, one B, one C, one H, one G, to size noted or to size required. If you build one cabinet, L can butt against A, Illus. 107. If a continuous base is preferred, notch A 3½ x 3¾'' instead of 3½ x 3'' specified. Hinge door with two fast-pin cabinet hinges for flush doors. Hold door closed with a magnetic catch. Hang door on right or left side. Fasten door pull.

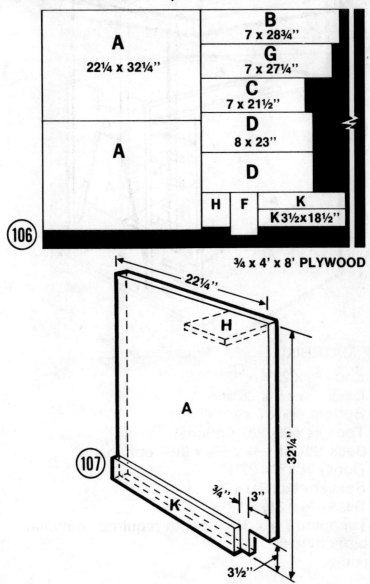

STORAGE CABINET AND TOTE BOX

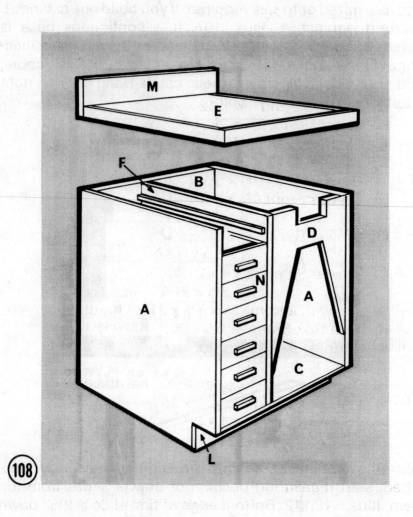

LIST OF MATERIAL

2 — **A** - End - ¾ x 22¼ x 32¼"
1 — **B** - Back - ¾ x 20½" x 28¾"
1 — **C** - Bottom - ¾ x 21½ x 20½"
1 — **D** - Front - ¾ x 12 x 23"
2 — **E** - Top - ¾ x 22 x 23" optional
1 — **F** - Divider - ¾ x 21½ x 28"
2 — **G** - Tote Box End - ¾ x 12 x 22"
1 — **H** - Spacer - ¾ x 5¾ x 7¾"
2 — **K** - Cleat - ¾ x 3½ x 18½"
1 — **L** - Toeboard - ¾ x 3½ x 22" optional
1 — **M** - Back Splash - ¾ x 5½ x 22" optional
6 — **N** - Drawer Front - ¾ x 4 x 7¾"
1 — "   "   "   ¾ x 3¼ x 7¾"
6 — **O** - Drawer Back - ¾ x 3¾ x 7¼"
1 — "   "   "   ¾ x 3 x 7¼"
12 — **P** - Drawer Side - ¾ x 4 x 21¼"
2 — "   "   "   ¾ x 3¼ x 21¼" - use 1 x 8
7 — **Q** - Drawer Bottom - ¼ x 7¼ x 21¼" hardboard
2 — **R** - Tote Box Side - ¾ x 5 x 20"
1 — **S** - Bottom - ¾ x 10⅜ x 20"
1 — Top - ¾ x 4 x 20"
14 — **U** - Drawer Slide - ¼ x ¾ x 21¼" hardboard
4 — **V** - Tote Box Cleat - ½ x ½ x 15"
8 — **W** - Drawer Pull - ¾ x 1 x 3"

Following cabinet assembly procedure previously described, start measuring position of drawer slides from top down, Illus. 110,112. Bottom edge of first slide is 2½" down from top. Next slide is 6½". Glue and brad each in position indicated to A and F.

Apply glue and nail K to A, A to BC; B and C to F; A and F to D, Illus. 108,114.

Position of F is shown, Illus. 108, 113.

The toeboard L can be continuous or cut to length required.

Cut parts for drawer to fit overall size space.

CUTTING DIAGRAM

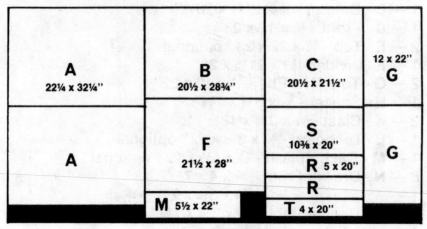

¾ x 4' x 8' PLYWOOD

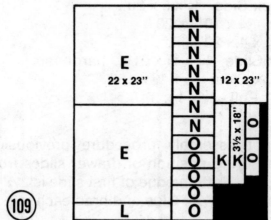

88

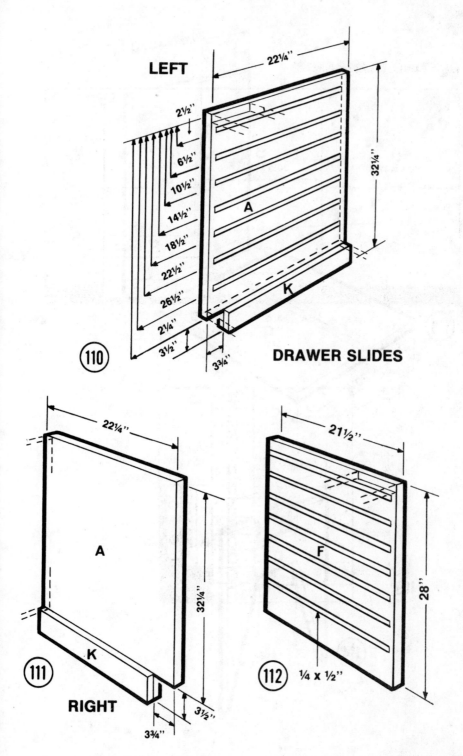

LEFT

22¼"

2½"

6½"

10½"

14½"

18½"

22½"

26½"

2¼"

3½"

3¾"

A

K

32¼"

DRAWER SLIDES

(110)

22¼"

A

K

(111)

RIGHT

32¼"

3½"

3¾"

21½"

F

(112) ¼ x ½"

28"

89

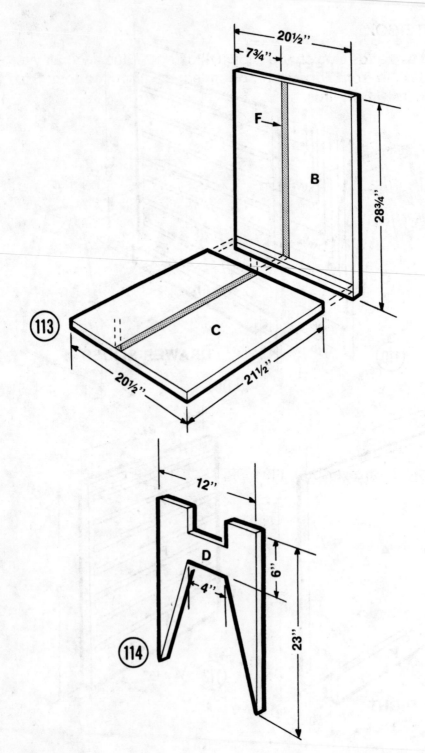

20½"

7¾"

F

B

28¾"

113

C

20½"

21½"

12"

D

6"

4"

23"

114

90

TOTE BOX

Cut two ends G to shape shown, Illus. 115. Glue and nail V to G, 1⅜" in from edge with bottom edge 5" from bottom; S to R; G to R,S,T, Illus. 116.

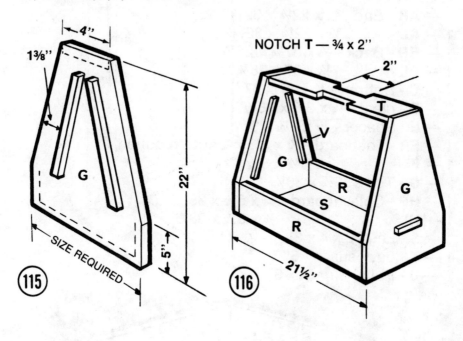

Apply 3" drawer pull, Illus. 99,100,101,116.

CORNER WORKBENCH

The revolving tool shelf in this workbench, Illus. 91, provides handy storage space for small tools, accessories, etc.

LIST OF MATERIAL

1 — **AR** - End - ¾ x 22¼ x 32¼"
1 — **AL** -   "   ¾ x 22¼ x 32¼"
1 — **BR** - Back - ¾ x 37¾ x 28¾"
1 — **BL** -   "   ¾ x 37 x 28¾"
1 — **C** - Bottom - ¾ x 37 x 37"
2 — **D** - cleat - ¾ x 3½ x 18½"
2 — **E** - Spacer - ¾ x 5¼ x 37"
1 — **FR** - Toeboard - ¾ x 3½ x length required
1 — **FL** -   "   ¾ x 3½ x   "   "
2 — **G** - Top - 38¼ x 38¼"*
1 — **HR** - Splashboard - ¾ x 5½ x 38½"
1 — **HL** -   "   ¾ x 5½ x 38½"
1 — **S** - Leg - 2 x 4 x 3½"
1 — **T** - Lazy susan - 6"
2 — **U** - Pulls - ¾ x ¾ x 3"

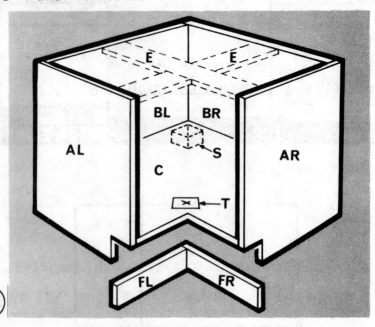

*for heavy duty use double thickness

REVOLVING UNIT

1 — **K** - ¾ x 36 x 27⅛"
1 — **L** - ¾ x 15 x 27⅛"
1 — **M** - ¾ x 20¼ x 26⅛"
1 — **N** - ¾ x 36 x 36"
4 — **O** - ¾ x 15 x 20¼"
1 — **P** - ¾ x 20¼ x 20¼"
1 — **R** - ¾ x 5¼ x 5¼"

Cut all inner parts to size assembled shell, Illus. 117, requires.
Illus. 118 provides an economical layout.

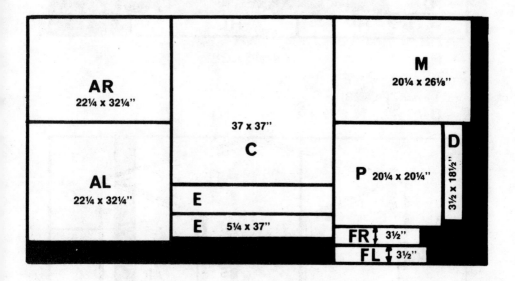

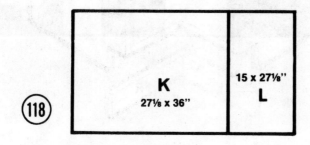

CUTTING DIAGRAM

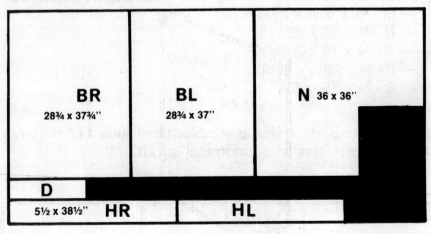

BR
28¾ x 37¾"

BL
28¾ x 37"

N 36 x 36"

D

5½ x 38½" HR

HL

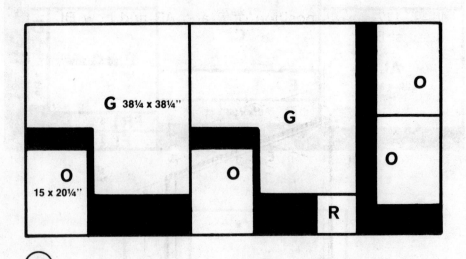

G 38¼ x 38¼"

G

O

O

O
15 x 20¼"

O

R

118

94

Nail cleats D, Illus. 119, in position to AL and AR.

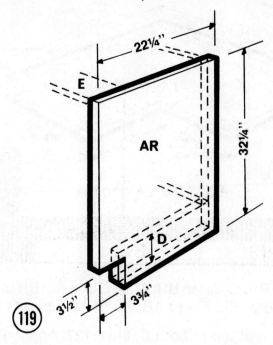

22¼"

E

AR

32¼"

D

3½"   3¾"

(119)

Illus. 117 shows position of E and AR and how BL butts against BR.

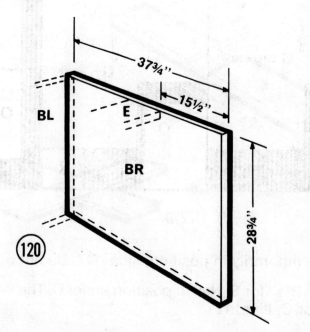

37¾"

15½"

BL   E

BR

28¾"

(120)

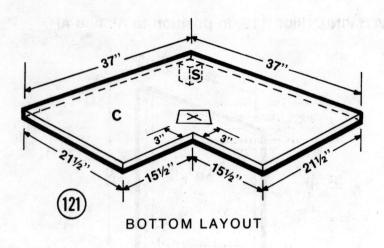

BOTTOM LAYOUT

Cut C to overall size shown, Illus. 121.

Glue and nail AR to C; AR to BR; AL to C and BL; BR to BL and to C; FR to end of FL; FR to AR; FL to AL, Illus. 117.

Cut a ⅜" deep half lap in both E, Illus. 122. Apply glue and screw half lap together, Illus. 122a, with ⅝" No. 6 flathead screws.

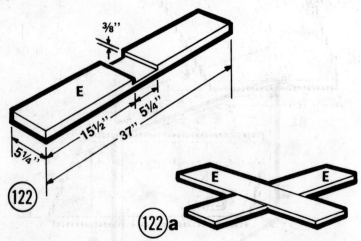

Screw E temporarily in position, Illus. 117. Do not use glue.

Cut 2 x 4 x 3½" for S. Nail in position under C. This acts as a support for C, Illus. 121.

96

REVOLVING UNIT

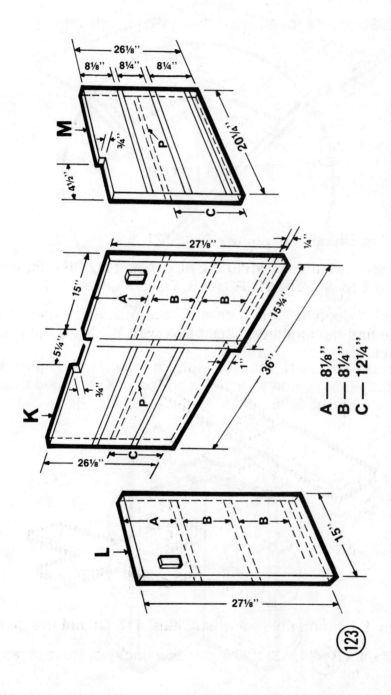

A — 8⅛"
B — 8¼"
C — 12¼"

Cut K, L and M, Illus. 123, to size indicated. Glue and nail K to L, Illus. 124.

Cut a 36" circle for N, Illus. 124. Saw 15" opening.

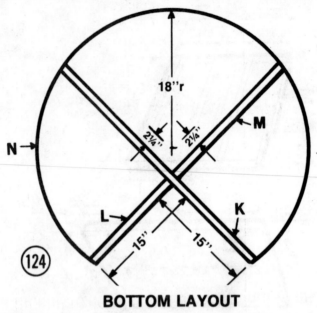

BOTTOM LAYOUT

Glue and nail L to N, Illus. 125. Bottom edge of L and right half of K project ¼" below N. Nail N to bottom of K on left side. Nail K to N on right side.

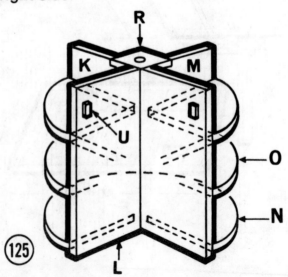

Cut R, Illus. 125, 128, 5¼ x 5¼". Apply glue and screw R to K and M; N to M.

Cut four O, Illus. 126, to size required. Glue and nail L and K, K and M to O, Illus. 123, 125.

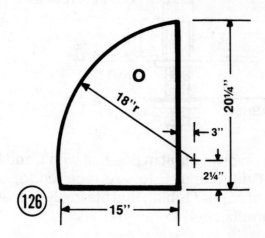

O

18"r

20¼"

3"

2¼"

(126)

15"

Cut one P to size required, Illus. 127. Glue and nail K and M to P in position noted, Illus. 123.

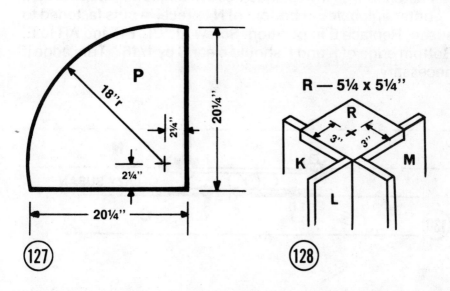

P

18"r

20¼"

2¼"

2¼"

20¼"

(127)

R — 5¼ x 5¼"

R

3" 3"

K M

L

(128)

Cut head off a ½ x 2" machine bolt, Illus. 129. Drill 9/16" hole through R. Countersink nut at top. Insert washer in position shown. Fasten bolt to R.

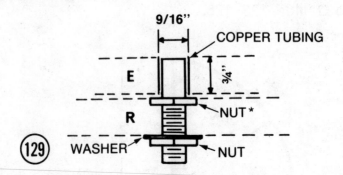

Remove E. Place revolving unit in position with L and K flush with edge of C. Drill hole in E to size required for a brass bushing or piece of copper tubing that fits freely over stem on bolt. Bushing permits shelf to revolve.

Place 6" Triangle or equal lazy susan on C in position noted, Illus. 121. Locate and drill four pilot holes for No. 6 self tapping screws.

Position susan on N, Illus. 130. Drill four 5/16" holes through N. Fasten four ¼ x 1" slotted head machine screws to susan. Countersink holes in bottom of N to receive nuts fastened to susan. Replace E in position. Screw AL, BL, BR and AR to E. Bottom edge of K and L should clear C by 1/16". Trim edge if necessary.

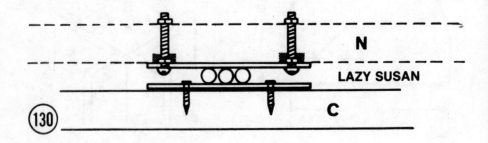

*Countersink

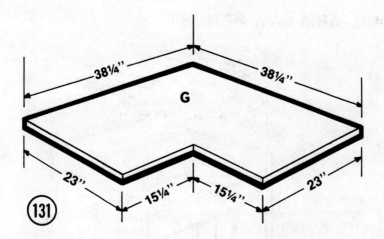

G

38¼" 38¼"

23" 15¼" 15¼" 23"

(131)

Cut a single or double thickness countertop to size shown or
to size required, Illus. 131, 132. Finish countertop with ⅛ or
¼" tempered hardboard.

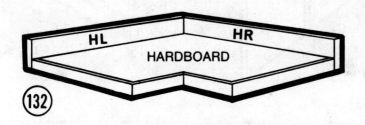

HL HR

HARDBOARD

(132)

RADIAL ARM SAW BENCH

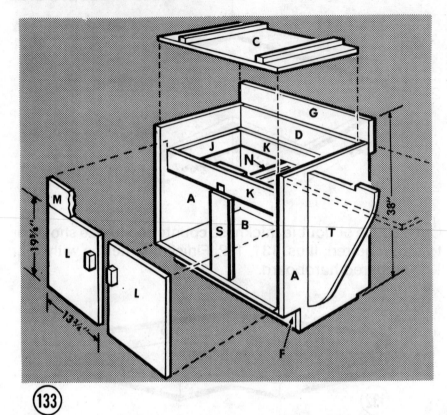

(133)

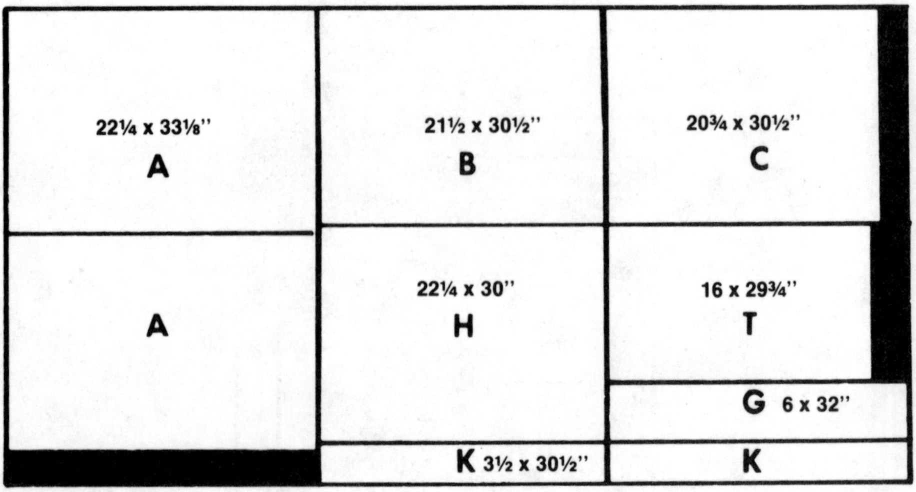

22¼ x 33⅛'' **A**	21½ x 30½'' **B**	20¾ x 30½'' **C**
A	22¼ x 30'' **H**	16 x 29¾'' **T**
		G 6 x 32''
	K 3½ x 30½''	**K**

(134)   ¾ x 4 x 8' PLYWOOD

LIST OF MATERIAL

2 — **A** - End - ¾ x 22¼ x 33⅛"
1 — **B** - Bottom - ¾ x 21½ x 30½"
1 — **C** - Saw Support - ¾ x 20¾ x 30½"
1 — **D** - Back - ¾ x 30½ x 29⅝"
2 — **E** - Cleat - ¾ x 3½ x 18½"
1 — **F** - Front Toeboard - ¾ x 3½ x 30½"
1 — **G** - Back Splashboard - ¾ x 6 x 32"
1 — **H** - Extension Table Leaf - ¾ x 22¼ x 30"
2 — **J** - Saw Support Framing - ¾ x 3½ x 19¼"
2 — **K** - " ¾ x 3½ x 30½"
2 — **L** - Door - ¾ x 13¾ x 19⅝"
1 — **M** - Front - ¾ x 5¼ x 30½"
1 — **N** - Framing - ¾ x 3½ x 20¾"
1 — **O** - " ¾ x 3½ x 5"
2 — **Q** - " ¾ x ¾ x 20¾"
1 — **P** - Lifting Lever - 1½ x 1½ x 24" hardwood
1 — **S** - Facing - ¾ x 3 x 19⅝"
1 — **T** - Table Support - ¾ x 16 x 29¾"
1 — Drill Rod - ¼ x 17½"
7 — Screw Eyes

Follow assembly procedure previously explained. Note cutting chart, Illus. 134.

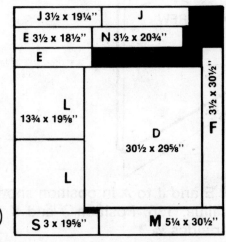

Notch ends A, ½ x 6", where noted, Illus. 135, if you wish to mount a lathe clamp, a saw accessory. Notch AE at bottom ¼ x 3" where indicated.

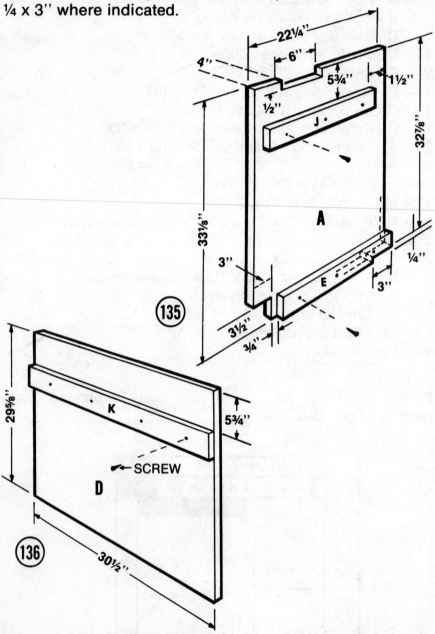

Glue and screw E and J to A in position shown, Illus. 135. Fasten K to D, Illus. 136. Position J and K to allow saw platform to clear sides ⅛".

Glue and nail ¾ x 1'' strips to C, Illus. 137, in position so they can butt against frame on saw.

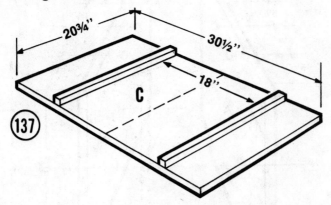

Glue and nail A to B and D, Illus. 133, 138; B to E; B to D; DK to J; K to J.

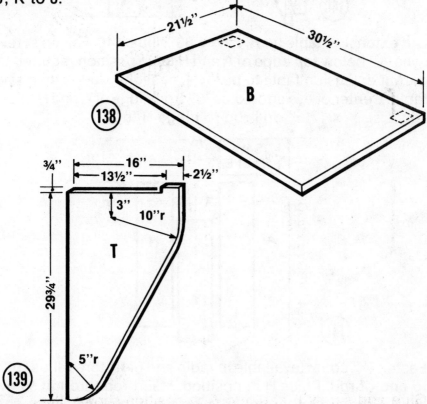

Cut extension table lid support T, size and shape indicated, Illus. 139. Notch top ¾ x 13½''.

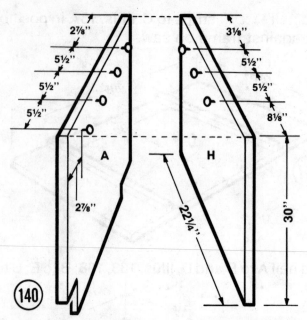

Cut extension table lid H, 22¼ x 30″, Illus. 140. Fasten screw eyes ⅜″ below top edge of A and H, or in position required to permit extension table to be level, or slightly lower than saw table. Center of eye should be ½″ from edge of A and H, Illus. 141. Use ¼ x 17½″ drill rod to hinge H to A.

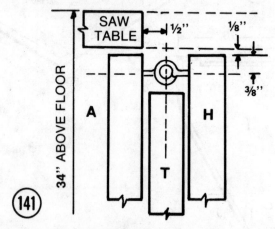

Fasten ¼″ collar, available in radio and hi-fi stores, Illus. 142, to end of rod. Place H in position. Insert rod through screw eyes. Fasten another collar to hold rod in place. Raise and brace H level. Fasten T to A with a pair of 3 x 2½″ butt hinges. Position T so it holds H level.

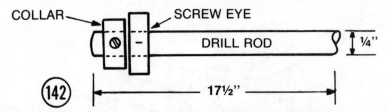

COLLAR — SCREW EYE

DRILL ROD

¼"

(142) ⊢——— 17½" ———⊣

Cut a piece of hardwood 1½ x 1½ x 24" for lifting lever P,
Illus. 143. Shape P as shown to make a handle. Drill hole 2"
from end to receive 2" No. 8 roundhead wood screw and
washer.

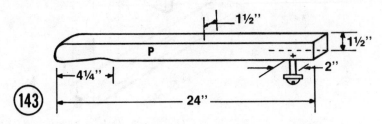

1½"

1½"

P

4¼"

2"

(143) ⊢——————— 24" ———————⊣

Saw a ¼ x 12" slot in N, Illus. 144.

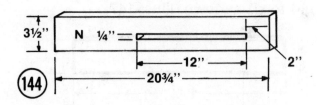

3½"

N ¼"

12"

2"

(144) ⊢——— 20¾" ———⊣

Saw a 1½ x 1½" notch in K and O, Illus. 145.

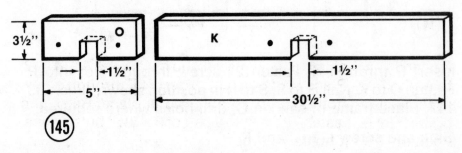

3½"

O

K

1½"

1½"

5"

(145) ⊢——————— 30½" ———————⊣

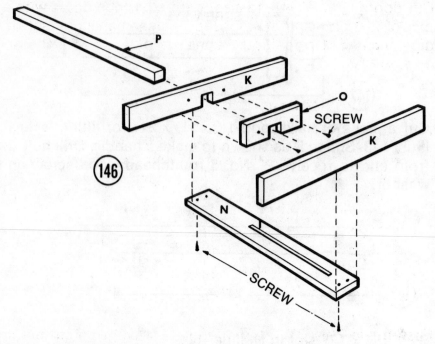

(146)

Glue and screw N to K, Illus. 133, 146.

Cut S and M to size shown, Illus. 147.

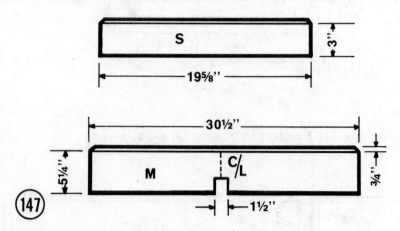

S

3"

19⅝"

30½"

5¼"

M

C/L

¾"

1½"

(147)

Insert P through K. Fasten 2" screw through slot into P. Fasten O to K. Nail B to S, S to N in position shown, Illus. 133, 147. Place frame of saw on C; drill holes where required.

Glue and screw C to J and K.

Cut doors L, Illus. 148, to size required. Hinge doors with a pair of fast-pin cabinet hinges for ¾ flush panel doors. Cut, glue and nail M in position. Fasten magnetic door catches to bottom of K.

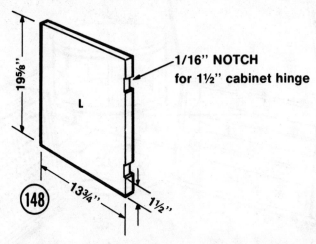

19⅝"

1/16" NOTCH
for 1½" cabinet hinge

L

(148) 13¾" 1½"

Fasten two 2½ x 3¼" high flat plate, swivel type casters to bottom of B, Illus. 138. To raise caster to 3½" height, fasten ¼" piece of plywood between plate and bottom of B. Bench is moved on two casters by lifting P.

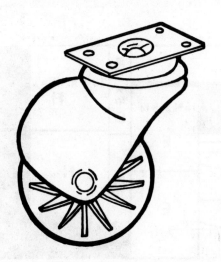

WALL CABINET WITH REVOLVING TOOL TURRET

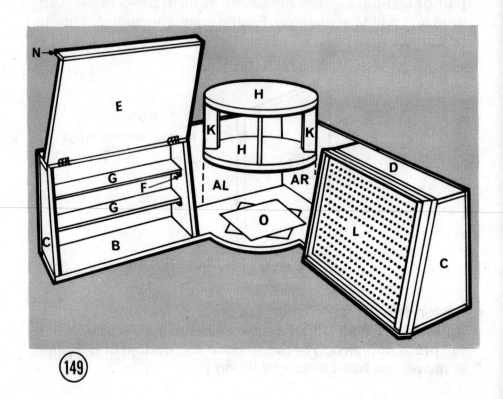

(149)

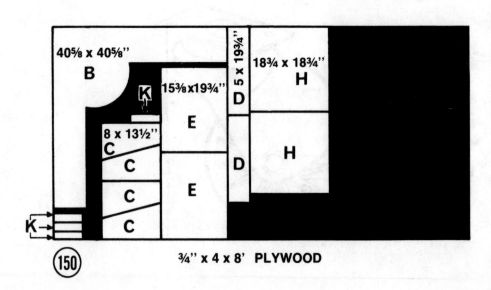

(150) ¾" x 4 x 8' PLYWOOD

LIST OF MATERIAL

1 — **AR** - Back - ⅜ x 15 x 41"
1 — **AL** -   "   ⅜ x 15 x 40⅝"
4 — **G** - Shelf - ⅜ x 5 x 18¼"
1 — **B** - Bottom - ¾ x 40⅝ x 40⅝"
4 — **C** - Side - ¾ x 8 x 13½"
2 — **D** - Top - ¾ x 5 x 19¾"
2 — **E** - Lid - ¾ x 15⅜ x 19¾"
8 — **F** - Shelf cleat - ¼ x ¾ x 5" hardboard
2 — **H** - Tool turret - 18¾ x 18¾"
5 — **K** - Tool Turret spacers - ¾ x 2 x 7"
2 — **L** - Tool panel - ⅛ x 14¼ x 18⅝" perforated hardboard
4 — **ML** - Frame - ¾ x 1 x 19¾"
4 — **MS** -   "   ¾ x 1 x 14⅝"
2 — **N** - Rest - ¾ x 1¾ x 19¾"
1 — **O** - 12" Lazy susan
2 — Brass mending plates, Illus. 157.
2 pairs cabinet hinges for ¾" doors.

Illus. 150 shows an economical layout for cutting parts from ¾ and ⅜" plywood.

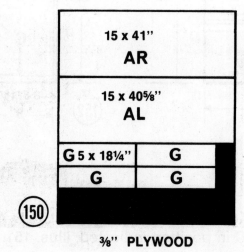

③⁵⁰ ⅜" **PLYWOOD**

111

Cut bottom B to size indicated, or desired, Illus. 151.

Cut ends C, Illus. 152. Glue and brad shelf cleats F to C in position shown.

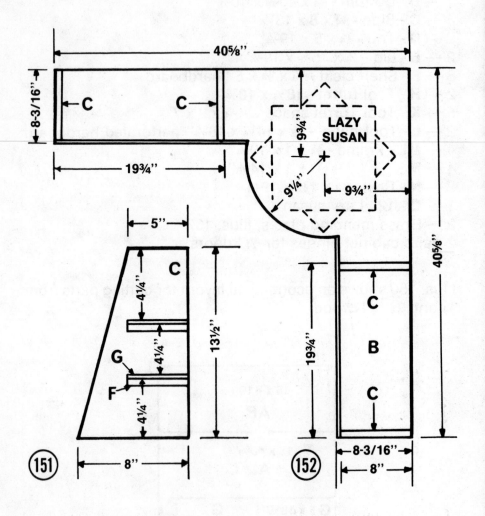

Cut back AR and AL. Glue and nail AR to B, AL to B, AR to AL; B, AL and AR to C in position indicated, Illus. 151.

Glue and brad shelves G in position, Illus. 149, 152.

112

Cut top D, Illus. 153, to size required. Notch for hinges selected.

Bevel front edge of D, Illus. 154, to angle required.

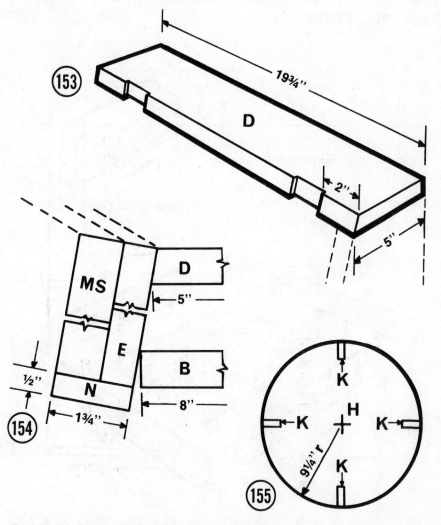

Cut E, N, Illus. 149, 158. Glue and brad N to E. Hinge E to D.

Cut two 18½" H, Illus. 155, for circular tool turret.

Install 12" lazy susan in position to B, Illus. 151, following procedure previously outlined.

Cut four K. Glue H to K. Fasten H to lazy susan.

Cut two ⅛ x 14¼ x 18⅝" perforated hardboard for L, Illus. 156.

Cut two ML, two MS from 1 x 2 cut to ¾ x 1". Cut rabbet in ML size indicated. Saw ⅛" slot in ML and MR 3/16" deep, ¼" from bottom edge.

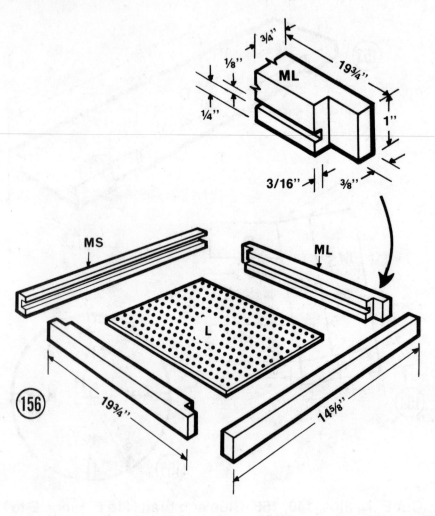

Apply glue and assemble L, ML and MS with four penny finishing nails.

Tool panel L can be held in position with one or two ½ x 1½"
brass mending plates, Illus. 157, fastened to ML. Fasten a No.
8 roundhead screw to E in position required. Saw head off
screw. The stud now permits lifting tool panel off. Fasten a
drawer handle to center of ML if you want to carry tool
panels, Illus. 158.

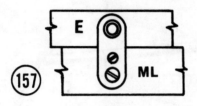

TOOL PANEL

CORNER UNIT

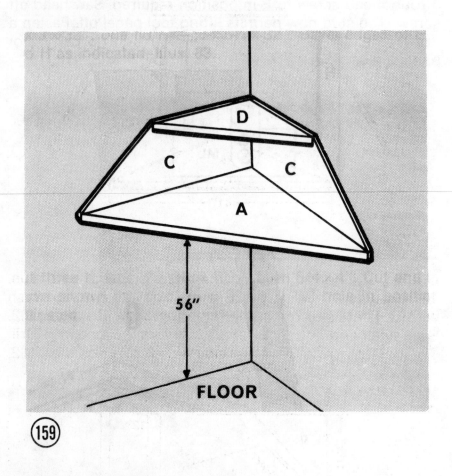

LIST OF MATERIAL

1 — ¾ x 4 x 4' plywood, A,B,D
1 — ⅜ x 16 x 48'' - C and tool holders

Position this cabinet about 56'' from floor. It provides storage for an electric drill, saber saw, sander, hand saw and other accessories.

Cut two C from ⅜'' plywood to size and shape shown, Illus. 160. Cut one A, one D from ¾'' plywood.

Glue and nail C to A and D, Illus. 159.

116

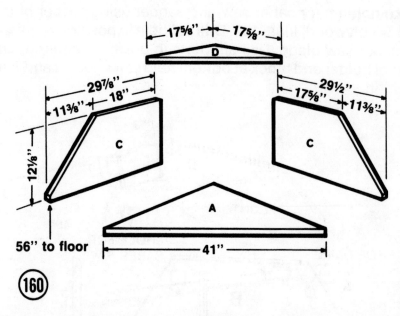

D

17⅝" — 17⅝"

29⅞"

11⅜" — 18"

29½"

17⅝" — 11⅜"

12⅛"

C

C

A

56" to floor

41"

(160)

Cut ¾" plywood to rough overall size required for B, Illus. 161. To determine size, place in position with top edge flush with D. Draw size required. Plane top edge 45°, Illus. 162. Saw sides and bottom to exact size to cover opening. Drill 1⅛" hole, or to size chuck on electric drill requires, Illus. 162.

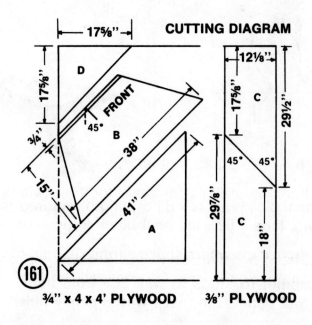

CUTTING DIAGRAM

17⅝"

12⅛"

17⅝"

D

C

29½"

FRONT

45°

B

¾"

38"

15"

29⅞"

45° 45°

41"

18"

A

C

(161)

¾" x 4 x 4' PLYWOOD

⅜" PLYWOOD

117

Make holders for saber saw and sander using spacer block and ⅜" plywood, Illus. 162. Drill ⅝" hole in position required for saber saw blade. Nail supports in position required. Lip on tool holder and block at bottom hold saw and/or sander in position.

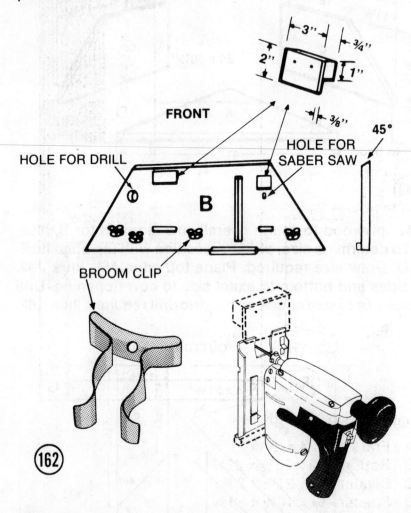

FRONT

HOLE FOR DRILL

HOLE FOR SABER SAW

B

BROOM CLIP

(162)

Saw vertical slot ½ or ¾ x 6" or length required to receive hand saws, Illus. 162. Nail heel block in position required.

Fasten broom clips where space permits to hold chisels, etc.

Fasten cabinet to studs in wall 56" from floor, or height desired. Nail panel B in place with 8 penny finishing nails.

118

LUMBER RACK ON CASTERS

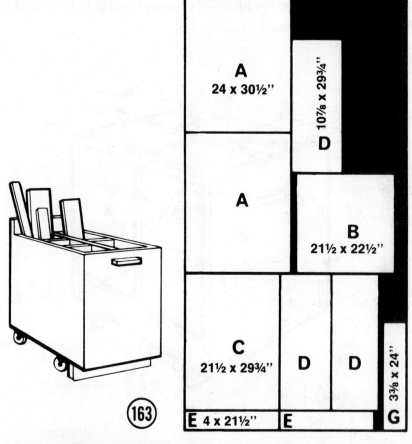

(163)

LIST OF MATERIAL

2 — **A** - End - ¾ x 24 x 30½"
1 — **B** - Bottom - ¾ x 21½ x 22½"
1 — **C** - Divider - ¾ x 21½ x 29¾"
3 — **D** - Spacer - ¾ x 10⅞ x 29¾"
4 — **E** - Rail - ¾ x 4 x 21½"
1 — **G** - Baseboard - ¾ x 3⅜ x 24"
1 pr. 2½ x 3¼" swivel casters
1 pr. 2½ x 3¼" fixed casters

Illus. 163 shows an economical layout for cutting parts from ¾ x 4 x 8' plywood.

119

The lumber rack can be built with plywood sides or with 4 x 21½" rails E, Illus. 164. If plywood is used, glue and nail plywood sides to ABD. Cut partition D to size required to butt against C. Notch D to receive E. Glue and nail C to D, E to D in position shown, Illus. 164.

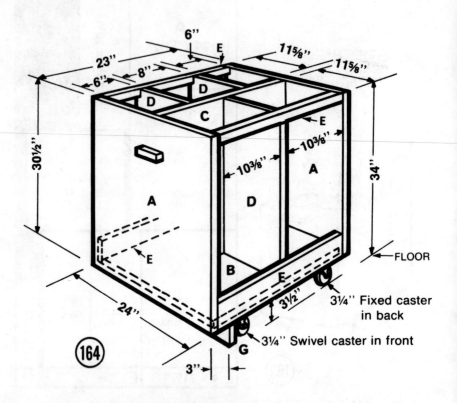

Cut ¼" plywood slightly larger than plate on casters. Glue and brad plywood to bottom of B. Screw swivel casters to front, fixed casters to back. Glue and nail B to baseboard G.

A wood or metal handle should be fastened to front end in position shown, Illus. 164.

120

6 DRAWER WORKBENCH WITH 6' VISE

(165)

This six drawer bench with two six foot vises, Illus. 165, is rated tops by schools, churches, juvenile and adult correctional institutions. If you need to submit a bid, be sure to mention price includes delivery.

LIST OF MATERIAL

4 — 2 x 4 x 12' - A,B,C,N
3 — 1 x 6 x 12' - D,E,F
1 — 1 x 6 x 6'
1 — 5/4 x 3 x 2' - G
1 — ⅛ x 4 x 4' pegboard - H,S
3 — 1 x 2 x 8' - K,R
3 — 2 x 8 x 6' - M
1 — 2 x 6 x 12' - P
4 — T,U - use ¾" plywood
1 — ¼ x 4 x 8' - V
18 — ¼ x 4" carriage bolts, nuts, washers*
2 — ½ x 6" machine bolts,   "   "
2 — ½ x 5"   "   "   "   "
24 — 2½" No. 10 flathead screws
108 — 1½"   "   "   "   "
24 — 1¼"   "   "   "   "
24 — 1¼"   "   "   "   "
108 — 1" No. 8   "   "
2 — 1" wood drawer pulls
2 — plunger type cabinet catches
12 — metal drawer pulls
¼ lb. 4 and 6 penny finishing nails
1 box ¾" brads
24 lineal ft. 1 x 1 steel angle L
2 prs. 1¼" offset fast pin hinges
    Pegboard hangers as required

Cut six legs A, Illus. 166, 2 x 4 x 32½". Notch A at top 1½ x 3½" to receive B. Notch a (1½ x 3½") 3⅛" up from bottom to receive B.

*¼" Teenuts and ¼ x 3½" cap screws or round head stove bolts can also be used.

TOP

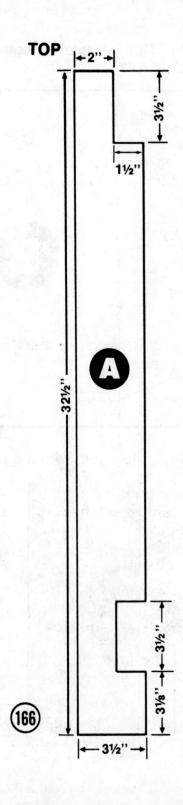

2"

3½"

1½"

32½"

Ⓐ

3½"

3⅛"

⑯⑥

3½"

123

Cut six B, 2 x 4 x 22¼". Drill ¼" hole through B at both ends, in position shown, Illus. 167.

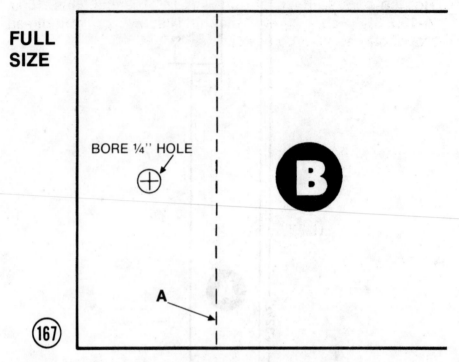

FULL SIZE

BORE ¼" HOLE

B

A

⑯⑦

Temporarily nail B to A, Illus. 168, with a 6 penny nail.

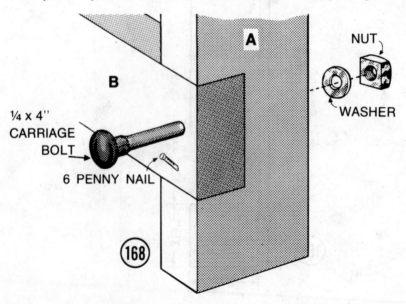

NUT

A

B

WASHER

¼ x 4"
CARRIAGE
BOLT

6 PENNY NAIL

⑯⑧

124

Using ¼" hole in B as a guide, drill ¼" hole through A. Fasten B to A with ¼ x 4" carriage bolts, nuts, washers, Illus. 169. Tighten nuts so head of bolt is flush. Teenuts, Illus. 169a, ¼-16 x 3½" cap screw, machine screw or roundhead stovebolt can also be used.

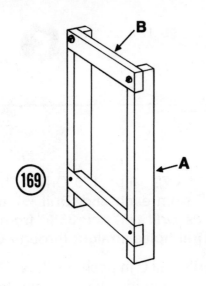

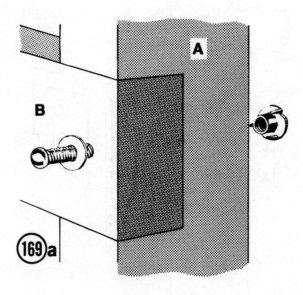

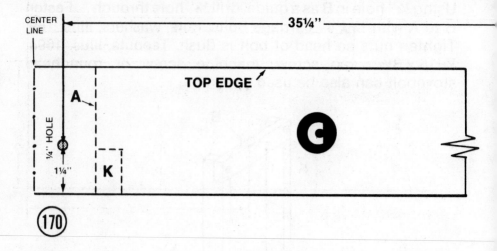

CENTER
LINE

A

¼" HOLE

1¼"

K

TOP EDGE

35¼"

C

(170)

Cut two rails C, 2 x 4 x 72", Illus. 170. Drill ¼" hole, 1¼" from bottom edge, 6⅜" from each end. Drill ½" hole, ⅞" from edge, 9⅜" from ends. Drill a ¼" hole 35¼" from right end of C to fasten C to A. Drill holes straight through C.

Clamp or temporarily nail C in position, Illus. 171, to A. Using ¼" holes through C as a guide, drill ¼" holes through A. Bolt C to A with ¼ x 4" carriage bolts and washers.

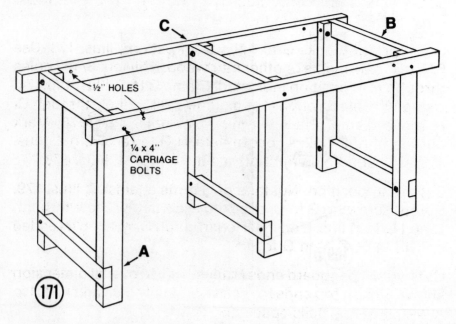

C

B

½" HOLES

¼ x 4"
CARRIAGE
BOLTS

A

(171)

126

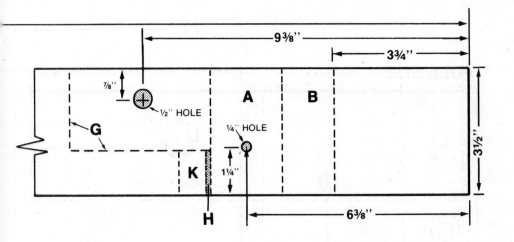

The bottom shelf can be made from two pieces of ¾" plywood or from 1 x 6 x 63" DEF. Notch two D, Illus. 172, to receive A. Drill six 3/16" holes through D in position indicated, ⅜" from ends and over middle B.

Cut one E and one F to exact width required, Illus. 173. Drill six 3/16" holes, ⅜" from ends, and centered over middle B. Cut F to width required after fastening E in place. Glue and screw D, E and F to B, Illus. 174, with 1½" No. 10 screws. Recess DEF ¾" from edge of B.

Cut four nut blocks G to full size of pattern, Illus. 175. Use 5/4 x 3" oak, maple or other hardwood. Drill four 3/16" holes through G in position indicated. Clamp G to C, Illus. 170,174. Using ½" hole through C as a guide, drill ½" hole through G. Remove clamp. Place ½" nut over hole, Illus. 176. Mark outline of nut. Chisel square hole in G to receive nut, Illus. 177. Chisel hole so nut finishes flush with G, Illus. 178.

Set nut in position. Nut face of G butts against C, Illus. 179. Before screwing G to C, check to ascertain ½" hole through C and G is in line. Bolt inserted through C must be threaded on nut in G. Fasten G to C.

Cut two ⅛" pegboard ends H, Illus. 180, to overall dimension shown. Notch top ends to receive G. Apply glue and nail H to A with 4 penny nails spaced 6" apart.

FULL SIZE

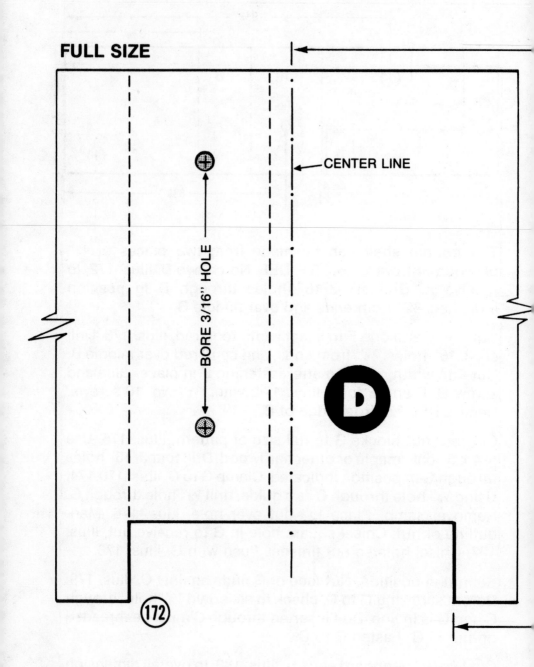

CENTER LINE

BORE 3/16" HOLE

D

172

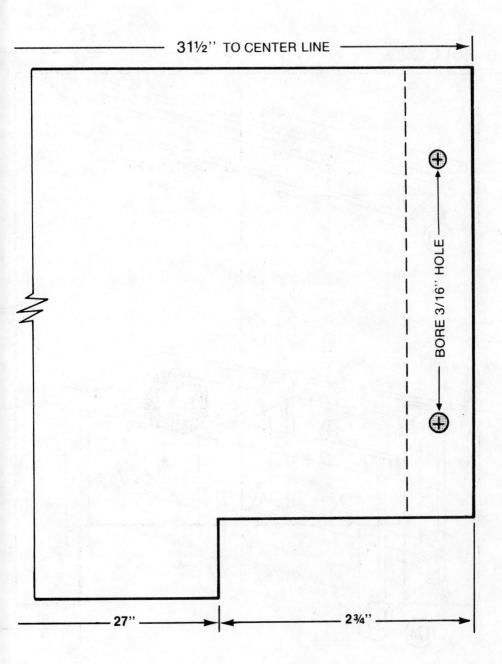

31½'' TO CENTER LINE

BORE 3/16'' HOLE

27''

2¾''

129

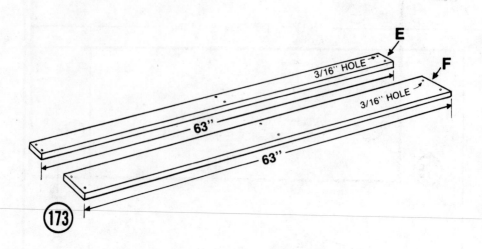

E

3/16" HOLE

F

3/16" HOLE

63"

63"

(173)

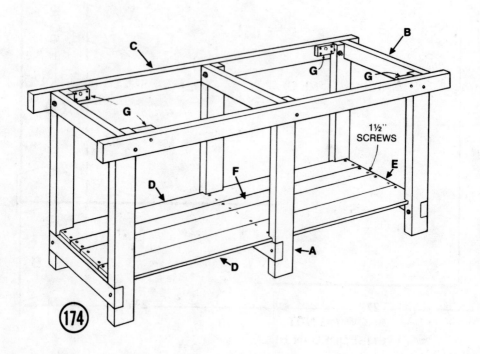

C

B

G

G

G

1½"
SCREWS

F

D

E

A

D

(174)

130

FULL SIZE

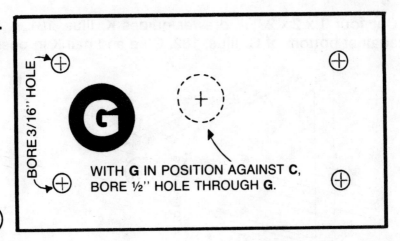

BORE 3/16" HOLE

G

WITH **G** IN POSITION AGAINST **C**, BORE ½" HOLE THROUGH **G**.

(175)

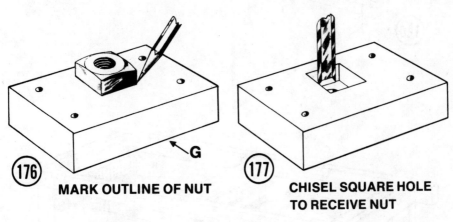

(176) **MARK OUTLINE OF NUT**

(177) **CHISEL SQUARE HOLE TO RECEIVE NUT**

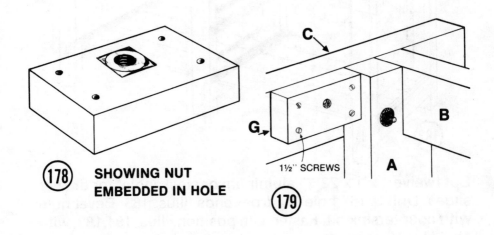

(178) **SHOWING NUT EMBEDDED IN HOLE**

C

G

1½" SCREWS

A

B

(179)

131

Cut four 1 x 2 x 22¼" drawer guides K, Illus. 181. K butts against bottom of G, Illus. 182. Glue and nail K in position.

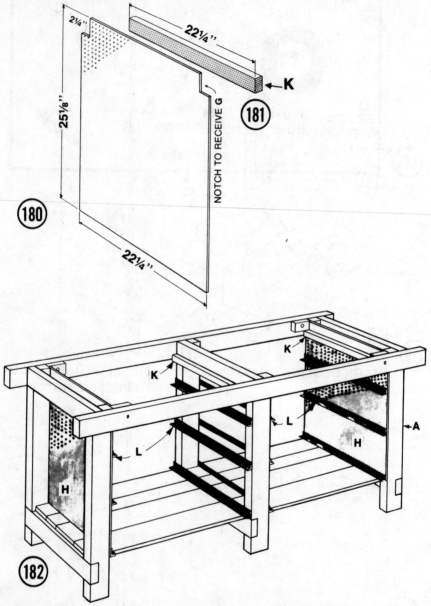

Cut twelve 1 x 1 x 22¼" aluminum or steel angle* for drawer slides. Drill 3/16" hole ¾" from ends, Illus. 183. Bevel hole with countersink bit. Fasten L in position, Illus. 184,182, with 1¼" No. 10 screws.

*Length should equal drawer

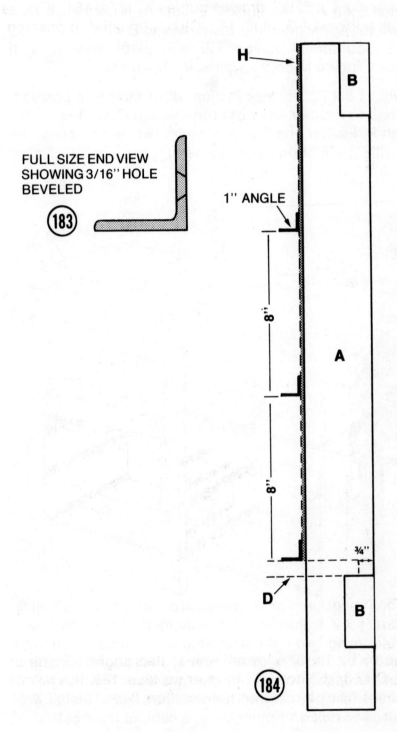

FULL SIZE END VIEW
SHOWING 3/16" HOLE
BEVELED
(183)

H

B

1" ANGLE

8"

8"

A

¾"

D

B

(184)

Cut three 2 x 8 x 72" M, Illus. 185. Cut one N from a 2 x 4 x 6 to 3" width. Apply glue and fasten MN to B with 2½" No. 10 screws. Countersink heads. Fill holes with wood filler. If necessary, plane M so it finishes flush with C.

Cut two 2 x 6 x 72" for vise P, Illus. 185. Clamp P in position. Use a nail to locate center of hole through G. Drill ½" holes through P. Fasten one P in place with two ½ x 5" bolts, the other with ½ x 6" bolts and washers.

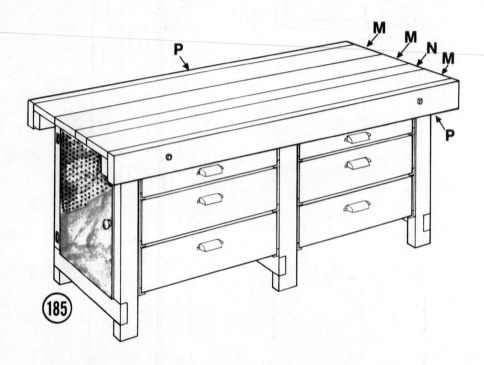

Cut two ⅛" pegboard or ¼" plywood panels for doors S, Illus. 186. Cut 1 x 2 frame to size indicated. Apply glue and assemble using two ⅝" corrugated fasteners at each joint. Glue and nail S to R with ¾" brads. Test door in opening. Plane or sandpaper to size required. Install door with a pair of 1¼" offset fast pin cabinet hinges, Illus. 186a. Install a 1" wood drawer pull and plunger type cabinet door catch.

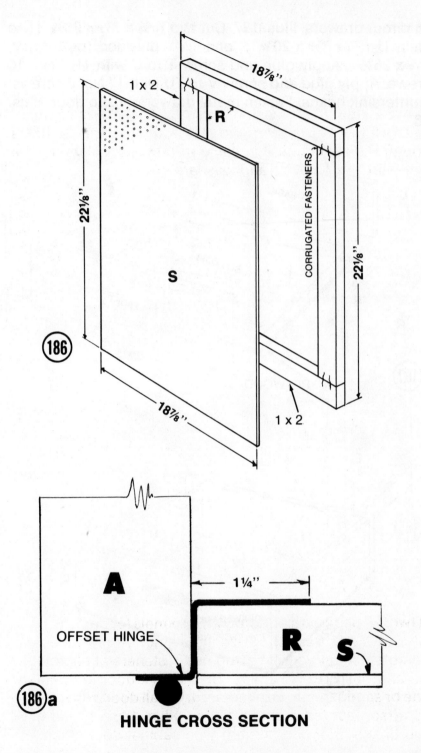

1 x 2

18⅞"

R

CORRUGATED FASTENERS

22⅛"

22⅛"

S

(186)

18⅞"

1 x 2

A

1¼"

OFFSET HINGE

R S

(186)a

HINGE CROSS SECTION

135

Build four drawers, Illus. 187. Cut two T, ¾ x 7½ x 26⅜''; two sides U, ¾ x 7½ x 20¾''; one ¼'' plywood bottom V, 22¼ x 26⅜''. Apply glue and screw T to U with 1½'' No. 10 screws. Apply glue and screw V to TU with 1'' No. 8 screws. Countersink heads. Fasten metal drawer pulls to door, Illus. 188.

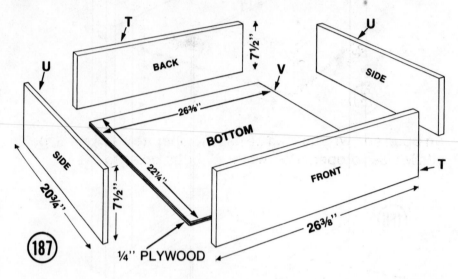

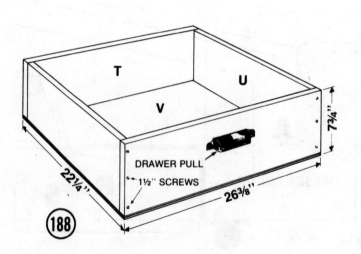

Build two top drawers, Illus. 189, following same procedure, to overall height of 4⅞".

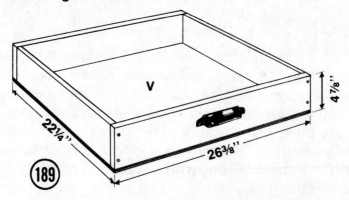

An open end wrench can be used to operate vise. The 5" bolts allow vise to open 1½" while 6" bolts open to 2½".

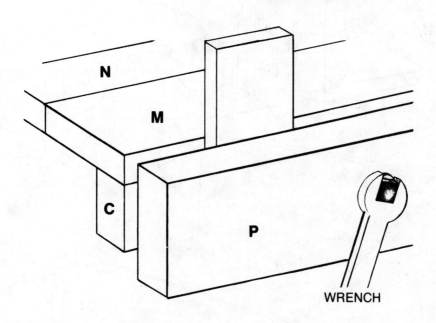

WRENCH

FOR FATHER, FOR CHILD

Encouraging a child to work with their hands, sparking an interest in woodworking, can pay a rich return in later years. Since this bench offers two vises, plus drawers that pull out from both sides, two can use it at the same time. Build a platform, Illus. 16, at a height that allows your child to comfortably use the vise. Allocate one end cabinet and drawer space for the child's tools. Always create a need where the child can assist in making every kind of project, repairing furniture, replacing a window or door screening. Creating an individual, one with an ability to enjoy time alone doing something they enjoy, is one of life's richest rewards.

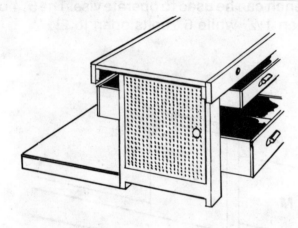

SWEDISH DOOR CHIMES

(190)

Hang this decorative chime, Illus. 190, on the inside of your outside door and it welcomes all who enter. Step by step directions plus full size decorating guides on foldout pattern insure professional results. This is an ideal gift. It proves a popular seller for those interested in earning income in their spare time.

LIST OF MATERIAL

1 — 1 x 6 x 2' clear pine for A,C,D
1 — ¼ x 1 x 2' fir plywood for B
1 — ¾ x 6" dowel for E
4 — 1¼" No. 8 oval head wood screws
4 — ¾" No. 6 roundhead   "   "
1 — B or second string for steel guitar
Orange shellac, glue, oak stain, paint.

Cut two A, 4⅝ x 11¾", Illus. 191. Use a coping, jig or saber saw to cut one half of a 7" opening.

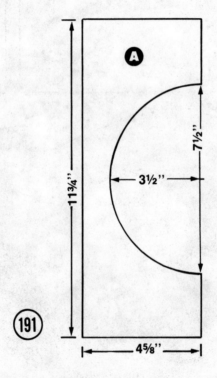

Cut two B, 9¼ x 11¾ from ¼" plywood, Illus. 192. Cut a 2¾" hole in top B in position indicated. Use an expansion bit or saber saw. Apply glue to contacting faces and assemble A and B in position shown, Illus. 193, 194.

140

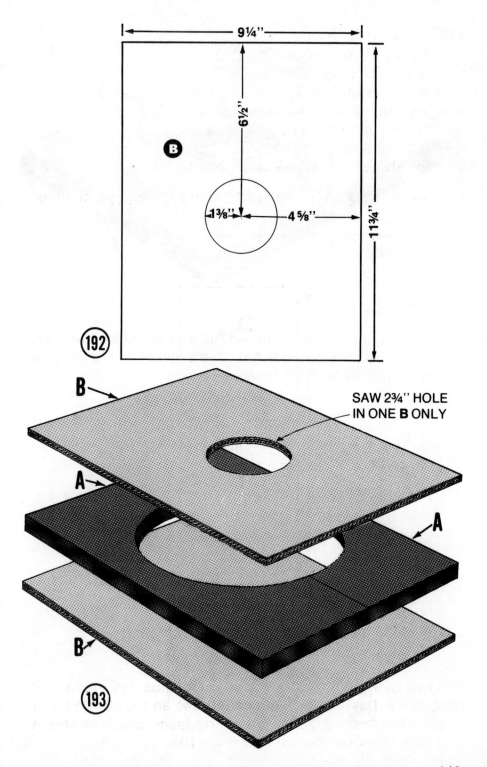

9¼"

6½"

B

1⅜" 4⅝"

11¾"

(192)

B

SAW 2¾" HOLE
IN ONE B ONLY

A

A

B

(193)

141

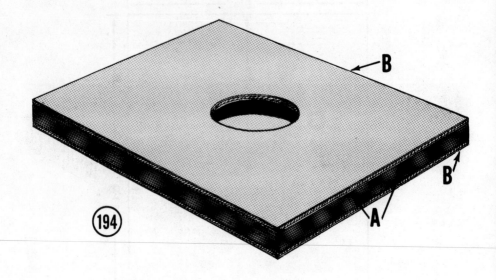

The design, Illus. 195, is printed full size on foldout pattern. Trace this on assembled B,A,B. Use a nail or awl to indicate position of 3/32 and ⅛'' holes.

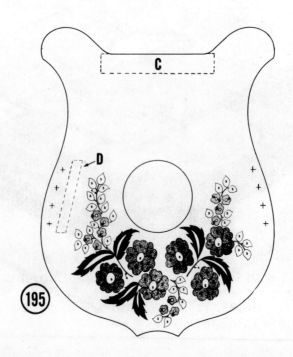

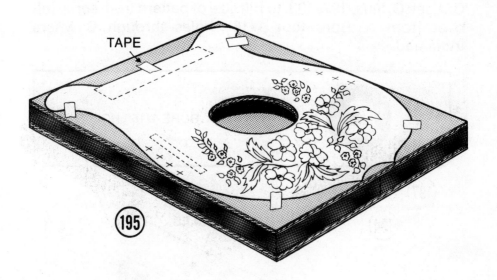

TAPE

(195)

Using a saber saw, cut assembled unit to shape shown, Illus. 196. Cut as close to drawn line as saw blade permits. File edges smooth using a half round cabinet file.

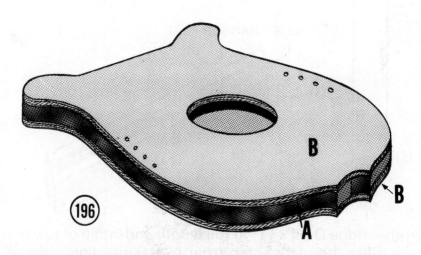

B

B

A

(196)

Finish edge with fine sandpaper wrapped around file.

Bore four ⅛" holes, ½" deep; four 3/32" holes, ⅜" deep where pattern indicates.

Cut one C, Illus. 197, 198, to full size of pattern from scrap left over from A. Bore four 1/16" holes through C where indicated.

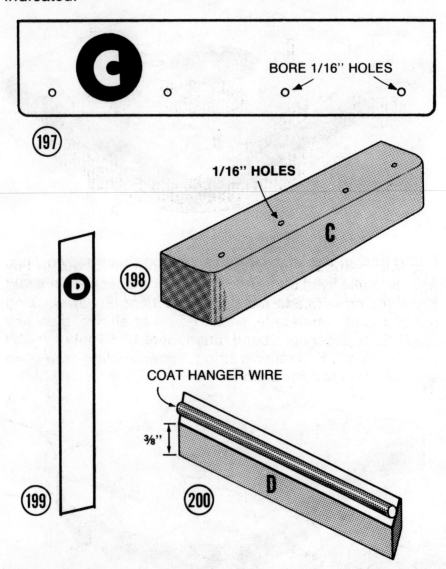

BORE 1/16" HOLES

⑲⑦

1/16" HOLES

C

⑲⑧

D

⑲⑨

COAT HANGER WIRE

3/8"

D

②⓪⓪

Cut one bridge D, ⅜ x ⅜" to full length and angle of pattern shown, Illus. 199. Use scrap from A. Make a slight sawcut down center of D.

Cut a 2¾" length of coat hanger wire, Illus. 200. Glue wire to sawcut.

Glue C and D to B, Illus. 201, in exact position shown on full size pattern. Clamp C and D in position until glue sets.

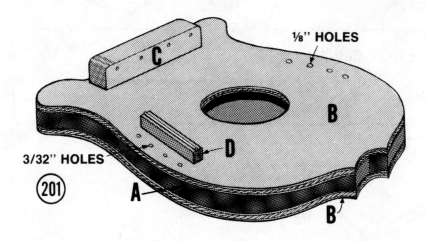

File four beads E, Illus. 202,203,204, from ¾" dowel, or buy four ¾" balls used on a child's playpen, blackboard or other toy. If you make beads, mark off ¾" sections on dowel. Using a half round cabinet file, shape dowel as shown, then saw apart. Sandpaper each bead round. Bore 1/16" hole through center of each E to receive string. Venetian blind draw pulls can also be used for beads.

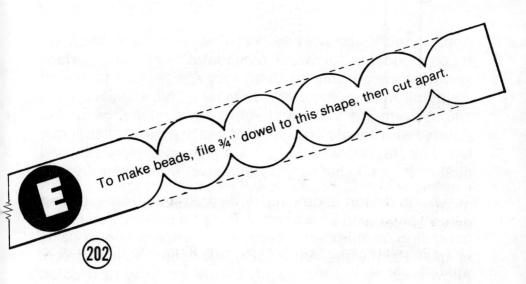

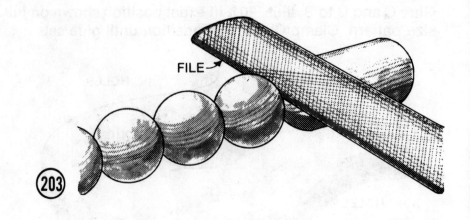

FILE

(203)

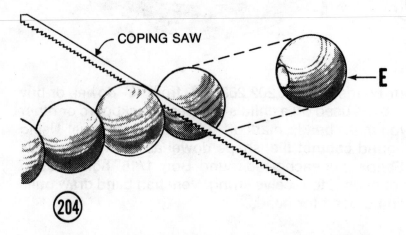

COPING SAW

E

(204)

Apply kind of finish desired. For a mellow, colonial finish, we recommend the following procedure. Sandpaper surface and edge smooth with very fine sandpaper. Apply light oak oil stain; follow manufacturer's directions. Rub stained project smooth with fine steel wool. Apply one coat orange shellac thinned with equal part alcohol. When dry, rub shellac lightly with fine steel wool so that gloss is removed. Apply a second coat of thinned shellac. Rub with steel wool when dry.

The floral design is optional. If desired, trace design using carbon paper and a hard pencil. Remove pattern. Paint color according to numbered color key. Use any good quality enamel. Paint white. Allow to dry, then apply #3 light green. Allow each to dry thoroughly before applying next color.

146

To string your chime, it's necessary to file a small section of the four 1¼" No. 8 oval head screws flat, Illus. 205. First drive screw into a piece of scrap. Fasten scrap in vise. File shank, then drill 1/32" hole through flattened area, Illus. 206. Drill same size holes through ¾" No. 6 oval head screws.

FILE SMALL SECTION OF SHANK FLAT

(205)

1/32" HOLE

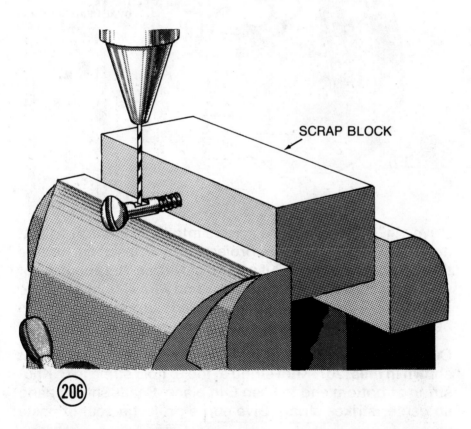

SCRAP BLOCK

(206)

We used a guitar B or second string. Cut two 9" and two 10" lengths. Use the 9" for two upper strings. Make small loop at one end of string and secure same to B with ¾" No. 6 roundhead screws, Illus. 207. Screw these all the way into B.

147

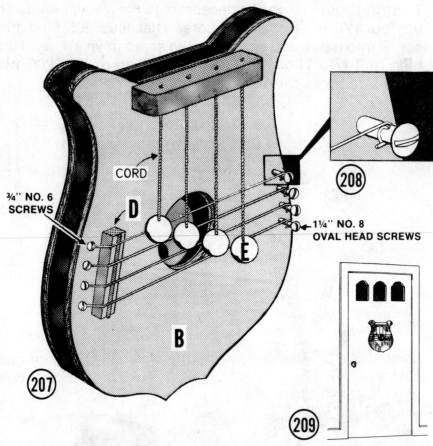

CORD

¾" NO. 6 SCREWS

D

E

1¼" NO. 8 OVAL HEAD SCREWS

B

207

208

209

Drive 1¼" No. 8 oval head screws into ⅛" holes in B so that approximately ⅝" of screw projects from B. Insert end of wire through hole in screw. Cut off end of wire so that about ½" of wire projects from hole in screw. Bend wire at right angle ⅛" from end. Turn screw so wire wraps around shank and becomes taut, Illus. 208.

Cut four lengths of nylon cord to position beads at height shown in Illus. 207. Knot string at top to hold string in C. Knot string at bottom end to keep E in place. Beads should hang so center strikes string. Give entire project a coat of paste wax.

Adjust 1¼" screws to "tune" chime to tone desired. Hang chime on door with regular staple type picture frame hanger, Illus. 209.

148

TOOL CHEST

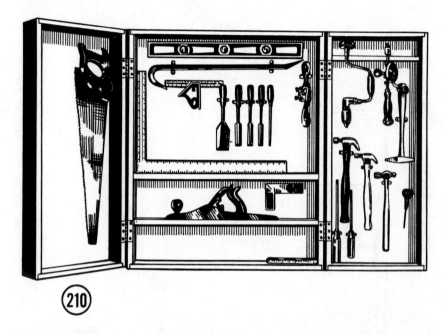

(210)

Regardless of your age, carpentry skill or number of tools you presently own, storing selected ones in this easy to build tool chest, Illus. 210, helps save time, temper and tools. When fastened to wall, the doors place tools within easy reach.

LIST OF MATERIAL

2 — 1 x 6 x 10' for A
1 — 1 x 4 x 10' for B,C
1 — 1 x 4 x 6' for F
1 — 1/8" x 3 x 6' pegboard
1 — 1 x 2 x 10'
24 — 2" No. 10 flathead wood screws
56 — 1¾" No. 10 ″   ″   ″
36 — ¾" No. 8   ″   ″   ″
3 prs. 2½" light butt hinges
2 — door pulls
2 — spring catches
1 — cabinet door lock

149

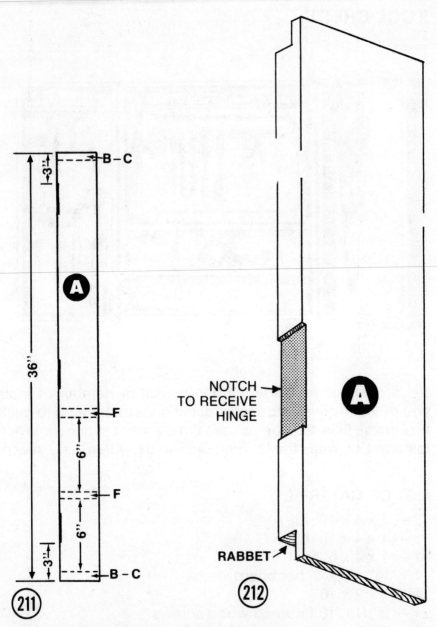

Cut six sides A - ¾ x 3½ x 36'', Illus. 211.

Saw rabbet at top and bottom of A, Illus. 212, to receive B or C. To visualize this rabbet, fold full size end of A along fold line, Illus. 213. Note position of notch for hinge. Do not notch or bore holes at this time.

150

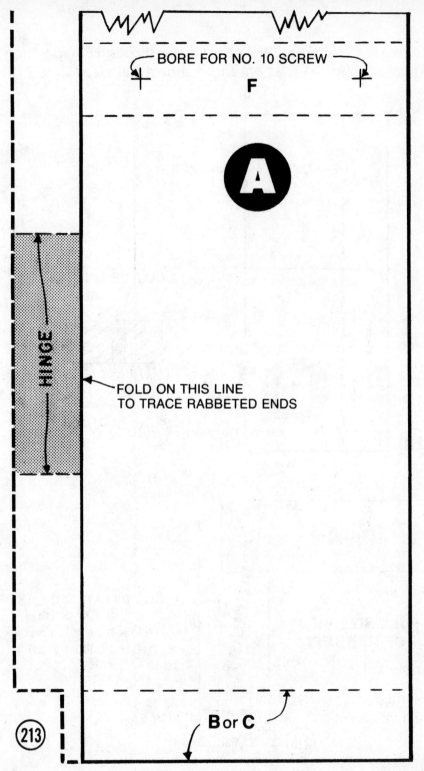

BORE FOR NO. 10 SCREW

F

A

HINGE

FOLD ON THIS LINE
TO TRACE RABBETED ENDS

213

B or C

151

Cut two B - ¾ x 3½ x 29½''. Bore holes through B in position indicated, Illus. 214, at an angle shown full size, Illus. 215.

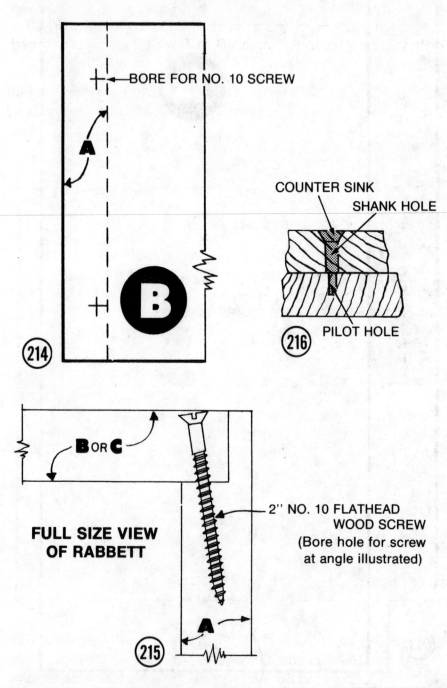

BORE FOR NO. 10 SCREW

A

B

COUNTER SINK

SHANK HOLE

PILOT HOLE

214

216

B OR C

FULL SIZE VIEW
OF RABBETT

2'' NO. 10 FLATHEAD
WOOD SCREW
(Bore hole for screw
at angle illustrated)

A

215

Apply glue and tack A to B with a few 1'' wire brads. Check assembly with a square and hold square with 1 x 2 nailed diagonally across. Using holes in B as a guide, drill pilot holes, Illus. 216, in A. Fasten B to A with 2'' No. 10 flathead screw. Countersink head. Fill hole with wood filler.

Cut four C, ¾ x 3½ x 14½'', Illus. 217. Drill holes in C, Illus. 215, at angle shown. Fasten C to A with 2'' No. 10 screws.

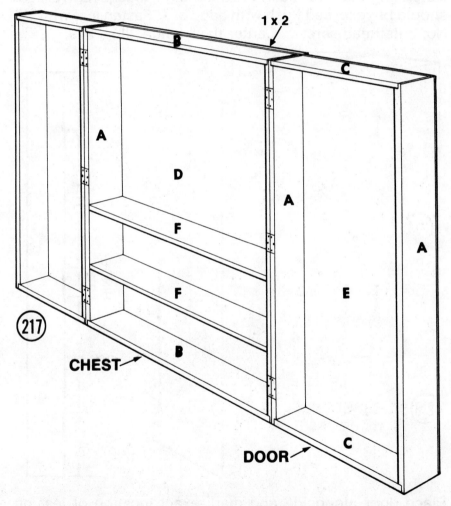

Cut back D, 30 x 36'' from ⅛'' pegboard. Apply glue and nail D to AB with 1'' brads. Drill holes through D about ⅜'' from edge and fasten D to AB with ¾'' No. 8 flathead screws spaced about 10'' apart.

153

Cut ⅛" pegboard, 15 x 36" for E, Illus. 217. Fasten E to A and C with ¾" No. 8 screws.

Cut two shelves F, Illus. 217, 213, ¾ x 3½ x 28½" or to length required. Drill holes through A in position shelf F requires. Apply glue and fasten A to F with 1" brads. Drill pilot holes in end of F and fasten A to F with 1½" No. 10 screws.

Notch edge of A to receive leaf of hinge, Illus. 212,218. Leaf should be recessed flush with edge of A. Fasten leaf with ¾" No. 8 flathead screws. Center third hinge, Illus. 219.

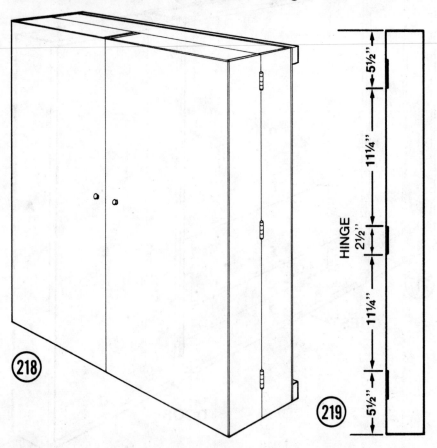

Place door alongside and mark exact location of leaf on door. Notch edge and screw hinge to door.

Apply door pulls and cabinet lock, Illus. 218, following manufacturer's directions.

154

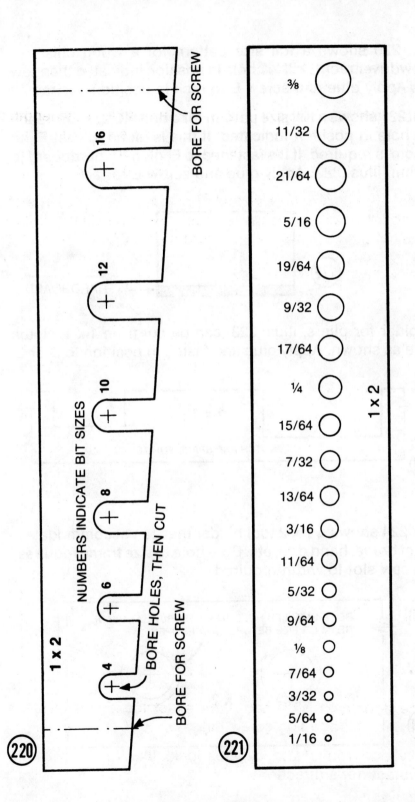

220

1 x 2

NUMBERS INDICATE BIT SIZES

BORE HOLES, THEN CUT

BORE FOR SCREW

BORE FOR SCREW

4   6   8   10   12   16

221

1 x 2

3/8
11/32
21/64
5/16
19/64
9/32
17/64
1/4
15/64
7/32
13/64
3/16
11/64
5/32
9/64
1/8
7/64
3/32
5/64
1/16

155

Illus. 220 shows a full size pattern for a wood chisel or screwdriver rack. Drill ¼" hole in position indicated then saw slot. Apply glue and screw E to rack in position desired.

Illus. 221 shows a full size pattern for a drill bit rack. Drill each size hole in position indicated. If this is glued to C or F, no bottom is required. If it's fastened to E, glue ⅛" hardboard to bottom, Illus. 222. Apply glue and screw E to rack.

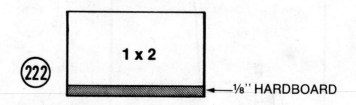

222

1 x 2

◄── ⅛" HARDBOARD

A holder for pliers, Illus. 223, can be cut from 1 x 1. Notch same as shown. Apply glue and fasten in position to D or E.

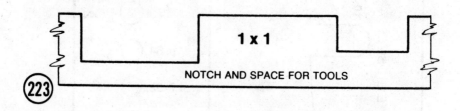

223

1 x 1

NOTCH AND SPACE FOR TOOLS

Illus. 224 shows a 1 x 2 tool holder that can accommodate a rachet brace, hand drill, etc. Bore hole to size frame requires, then saw slot to width required.

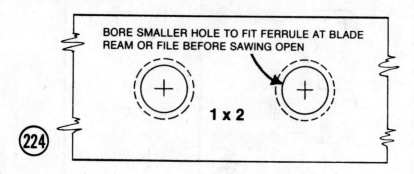

BORE SMALLER HOLE TO FIT FERRULE AT BLADE
REAM OR FILE BEFORE SAWING OPEN

1 x 2

224

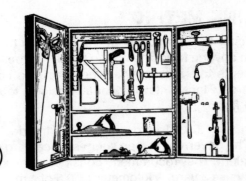

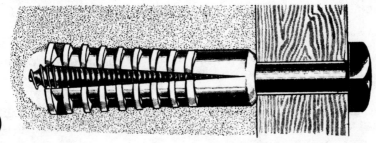

All tools can be hung with screw hooks, tool holders, or broom clamps.

Fasten chest to two 1 x 2 nailed horizontally at top and bottom across three studs. Use four ⅜ x 2½" lag screws and washers.

If you fasten chest to a masonry wall, use expansion shields or bolts, Illus. 225.

HOW TO THINK METRIC

Government officials concerned with the adoption of the metric system are quick to warn anyone from attempting to make precise conversions. One quickly accepts this advice when they begin to convert yards to meters or vice versa. Place a metric ruler alongside a foot ruler and you get the message fast.

Since a meter equals 1.09361 yards, or 39⅜"+, the decimals can drive you up a creek. The government men suggest accepting a rough, rather than exact equivalent. They recommend considering a meter in the same way you presently use a yard. A kilometer as 0.6 of a mile. A kilogram or kilo as just over two pounds. A liter, a quart, with a small extra swig.

To more fully appreciate why a rough conversion is preferable, note the 6" rule alongside the metric rule. A meter contains 100 centimeters. A centimeter contains 10 millimeters.

As an introduction to the metric system, we used a metric rule to measure standard U.S. building materials. Since a 1 x 2 measures anywhere from ¾ to 25/32 x 1½", which is typical of U.S. lumber sizes, the metric equivalents shown are only approximate.

Consider 1" equal to 2.54 centimeters; 10" = 25.4cm.

To multiply 4¼" into centimeters: 4.25 × 2.54 = 10.795 or 10.8cm.

INCH	—	MILLIMETER
1"		25.4
15/16		23.8
7/8		22.2
13/16		20.6
3/4		19.0
11/16		17.5
5/8		15.9
9/16		14.3
1/2		12.7
7/16		11.1
3/8		9.5
5/16		7.9
1/4		6.4
3/16		4.8
1/8		3.2
1/16		1.6

INCHES	—	CENTIMETERS
1		2.54
1/8		2.9
	1/4	3.2
3/8		3.5
	1/2	3.8
5/8		4.1
	3/4	4.4
7/8		4.8
2		5.1
1/8		5.4
	1/4	5.7
3/8		6.0
	1/2	6.4
5/8		6.7
	3/4	7.0
7/8		7.3
3		7.6
1/8		7.9
	1/4	8.3
3/8		8.6
	1/2	8.9
5/8		9.2
	3/4	9.5
7/8		9.8

4			10.2
	1/8		10.5
		1/4	10.8
	3/8		11.1
		1/2	11.4
	5/8		11.7
		3/4	12.1
	7/8		12.4
5			12.7
	1/8		13.0
		1/4	13.3
	3/8		13.7
		1/2	14.0
	5/8		14.3
		3/4	14.6
	7/8		14.9
6			15.2
	1/8		15.6
		1/4	15.9
	3/8		16.2
		1/2	16.5
	5/8		16.8
		3/4	17.1
	7/8		17.5
7			17.8
	1/8		18.1
		1/4	18.4
	3/8		18.7
		1/2	19.1
	5/8		19.4
		3/4	19.7
	7/8		20.0
8			20.3
	1/8		20.6
		1/4	21.0
	3/8		21.3
		1/2	21.6
	5/8		21.9
		3/4	22.2
	7/8		22.5
9			22.9
	1/8		23.2
		1/4	23.5
	3/8		23.8
		1/2	24.1
	5/8		24.4
		3/4	24.8
	7/8		25.1
10			25.4
	1/8		25.7
		1/4	26.0
	3/8		26.4
		1/2	26.7
	5/8		27.0
		3/4	27.3
	7/8		27.6

11			27.9
	1/8		28.3
		1/4	28.6
	3/8		28.9
		1/2	29.2
	5/8		29.5
		3/4	29.8
	7/8		30.2
12			30.5
	1/8		30.8
		1/4	31.1
	3/8		31.4
		1/2	31.8
	5/8		32.1
		3/4	32.4
	7/8		32.7
14			35.6
16			40.6
20			50.8
30			76.2
40			101.6
50			127.0
60			152.4
70			177.8
80			203.2
90			228.6
100			254.0

FEET = INCHES = CENTIMETERS

FEET	INCHES	CENTIMETERS
1 =	12 =	30.5
2 =	24 =	61.0
3 =	36 =	91.4
4 =	48 =	121.9
5 =	60 =	152.4
6 =	72 =	182.9
7 =	84 =	213.4
8 =	96 =	243.8
9 =	108 =	274.3
10 =	120 =	304.8
11 =	132 =	335.3
12 =	144 =	365.8
13 =	156 =	396.2
14 =	168 =	426.7
15 =	180 =	457.2
16 =	192 =	487.7
17 =	204 =	518.2
18 =	216 =	548.6
19 =	228 =	579.1
20 =	240 =	609.6

INDEX TO MONEY-SAVING REPAIRS, IMPROVEMENTS, PATTERNS AND BOOKS
(Number designates EASI-BILD Pattern or Book)

Acoustical Ceiling
609,613,615,665,684,685
Acoustical Fabric 612
Acrylic 607,611,694
Adapter
  electrical 664,694
  fireplace pipe 674
  plumbing pipe 675,682,685
  sound system 612
Add-a-Room 609
Adhesives
  carpet 683
  ceramic tile 606
  fiber glass panel 611,631,696
  floorcovering 606,615,665,683,685
  furniture 623,753,761
gluing reference guide 623
  ironwork repair 617,685
  paneling 605,615,665,684,685
  plastic pipe 675,682
  seam sealer 683
  wood flooring 685
Aerators, faucet 675
Air Cooler, window 135
Air Conditioner
  framing 632,665,685,773
Airplane, see Toy
Alarm devices 695
  automatic telephone dialer, bell,
  burglar, emergency, floodlight,
  fire sensor, garage door, panic,
  buttons, perimeter alarm, photo,
  electric eye,   smoke detector,
  under carpet mat, ultrasonic alarm
Alphabet, easy to trace 607
Aluminum
  binder bars 683
  carpet grippers 683
  flashing 603,607,609,613,632,649,
  foil insulation 632,685
  footing scaffold 696
  gutters 613,632,679,684,781
  hinges 751
  leader pipe 679,697
  louver 632,649,665,679,697,763
  moldings 605
  ridge 684
  roofing panels 679,680,684,696,
  siding 684,696
  skylight frame 696
  sliding door track 658
  spikes 613,679,696
  square tubing 658,672
  storm window 632
  tackless strips 683
  termite shield 609,632,679,697
  traverse rod 627
  vent 613,665
  washers 751

windows 603,613,623,632,685
window casement 632
Amplifiers 612
Anchor bolts 84,609,611,613,615,
  clips 611,632,679,697
Animal Cages 751
Answering Systems, telephone 695
Anti-Freeze
  toilet 675,682,685
Antiquing 623,761
Anti-theft Chains 695
Apartment, garage 763
Appliance Centers 3,243,244,245,
Apron, window 605,609,679,685
Arbor, router 615,761
Armchair Repair 623
Asbestos
  board 697
  roofing 696
Ash Pit 674
Asphalt roofing 609,663,685,696,763
Asphalt Tile 615,665,773,685
Astragal 611
Athletic Equipment 152,153,154
Attic Modernization 603,665,773
  built-in lighting 694
  stairways 615,665,763,773
  ventilators 609,613,631,665,682,
Auger Bits 694,753,754,761
Automatic Timer 694
Auxiliary Power Generator 694

Baby Cradle 761
  doll 753
  match cradle 756
Backing Board 682,685
Ballcock, toilet 675
Balustrade, dollhouse 753
Bar bookcase 690
  buffet 718
  cabinet 690
  colonial tavern 612
  playroom, record cabinet,
  revolving cabinet 690
  revolving shelf 508
  room divider 658
  sink, TV 690
  storage 605
  table 140
  wall 612
Barbecue 316,668
Barge boat 77
Barn, Red 679,680
  doors 679,680
  tool house 679
Barnyard Pulltoys 79,756,771
Base cabinet 3,191,243,244,245,608,
Baseboard 605,609

Basement, house 632
Basement Modernization 615
  carpeting 683
  drapery 605
  electrical wiring 615,694
  family room 615
  greenhouse entry 611,615
  luminous ceiling 615,694
  outside entry 615
  paneling 605,615
  plyscord decorations 615
  partitions 615,632
  stairs 615,632,773
  sump pump 615,617,685
  tile floors 606,615,685
  waterproofing 615,617,632,685
  windows 615
Bathroom Accessories
  bathtub beauty bar 327
  bathtub repairs 675,685
  cabinets 158,606
  carpeting 683
  fiber glass bathtub, toilet 682,685
  fixtures 675,682
  floors 606
  lavatory enclosure 158,606
  lighting fixtures 694
  medicine chest repair 694
  plumbing wall 682,685
  sealants 606
  sinks 675,682,685
  telephone shower 682
  tiles 606
  toilet repair 675,685
  vanity 606
  ventilator 682
Bathroom Installation 682,685
  bathtub, fiber glass bathtub,fit-
  tings, lavatory, medicine cabinet,
  plumbing tree, plumbing wall,
  prefab bathroom unit, septic tank,
  shower, toilet.
Batter boards 609,631,632,663,679,
Battery
  alarms 694,695
  dollhouse lighting 694,753
  floodlights 694,695
Beds and Bunks
  colonial under eaves rope 68,761
  colonial crib 761
  dollhouse colonial cradle 753
  dollhouse rope spring bed 753
  double-deck 87,771
  hedboard 126
  houseboat 676
  studio 623,633
  under bed storage 634,792
Bell Alarm 694,695
  door 694

Benches
  cobbler's 102A,586,756,761
  colonial 23,586,761
  dollhouse cobbler's bench 753
  dining 307
  fireside 23,761
  lawn 325
  peasant 57
  work 672,677
Bi-fold Door, closet 605,634
Binders, carpet 683
Birdhouses, Feeders 669,756
  bluebird 110,669
  feeder 9,669
  martin 669
  Swedish 10
  wren 11,111,669,756
Bits
  auger 694,753,754,761
  countersink 761
  drill 613,684,761
  screwdriver 761
Blackboard
  kitchen message center 313,578
  play table 117
Blanket Storage 761,792,962
Bluebird House 110,669
Boards
  bed 126
  bulletin 93,607
  fence 607,631,781
  memo 313
Boats
  barge or pram 77
  cartop float 247
  houseboat 676
  kayak 317,757
  rowboat 77,85
  sail,centerboard 194
  sail scooter 248
  surfboard 247
  toy 60,67,72,771
Body Harnes
  roofing 696
Bookcases 271,605,612,658,664,
  690,761
  acrylic 792
  built-in 612,664
  corner 664
  desk 18,761
  dollhouse 753
  free standing 664
  record 192,664,690,792
  room divider 658,664
  window 271,605,627,664
Bookends 756
Bookshelves
  all purpose 6
  applique 756

duncan 35,761
  hanging 21
Bow Window
  bonnet 609,668
Breaker Switches 694
Breezeway
  how to build 910
  how to screen 613,781
Bricklaying 668,674
  barbecue 316,668
  fireplace 674
  mortar 668,674
  patios 668
  tools 668,674
  tree well 668
  walks 668
  walls 668,685
  veneering 668
Bridging 603,609,613,615,632,663,
Broom Closet 156,672
Buffet
  bar 718
  dining 138,718
Buildings, see Garage, Houses,
  Forms, Footings, Framing,
  Foundations, Kennel, Toolhouse,
  Stable.
Built-In
  bookcases 612,664
  cabinets 608,658,761
  closet 605,615
  cornice 605,627
  counter range 608,658,685
  fireplace 674
  hi-fi, stereo 612
  lighting 694
  range 608,658,685
  record storage 612,658
  refrigerator 608,658,685
  sewing center 672
  sink 608,658,685
  storage units 605,672
  wall to wall 664
Built Up Roofing 696
Buffet Bar 718
Bulletin Board 93
  outdoor 607
Bungalow, see cabins
Bunks, see beds
Burglar Alarm Installation 695
Bushings
  electrical 694
  plumbing 675

Cabana 663
Cabinets
  acrylic corner 792
  base 3,191,243,244,608,658
    685,761

  bathroom 158,606
  broom 156,672
  built-in 608,658,685,761
  cleaning utensil 156
  contemporary 658
  corner 38,753,792
  dollhouse corner 753
  end table 141
  fishing rod 630
  freestanding 658
  furniture 658
  gun 266,630
  hi-fi 272,612
  kitchen 243,244,245,246,608,
    658,685
  linen 634
  radial arm saw 672
  record 192,436,658,690
  sewing 543,672
  stereo 612
  storage 605,634
  tool 672,677
  trainboard 190,672
  wall acrylic 792
  wall hanging 24,608,658
  wall to wall 191,912,605,608,612,
    658,664,719
  wine storage 608,634

Cabins, Cottages 51,84,91,632,684
Cages 751
  catpartment, cavy, guinea pig,
  hamster, kennel, parakeet, rabbit
Calking, also caulking 613,668,675,
Camper 594
Cane Webbing 623
Canned Goods Storage 770,608,634
Canopy 305,607
Canvas Deck 613,781
Canvas Covered Kayak 757
Cape Cod House 514
Cari-Car 583
Carpeting 683
Carport 273,680
Carriage, stairs 603,615,617,632,
  763,773
Casement Windows 609,613,781
Casing 605,609,763,773
Cast Iron Pipes 675,679,682
Cat Entry 724,751
Catpartment 751
Caulking, also calking 613,682
Cavy Cage 751
Cedar Room 265 605
Ceiling Joists 603,609,613,615,632,
Ceiling,suspended 609,613,615,665,
  684,685
Ceiling Trim Plate 674
Ceramic Tile 606

how to lay, repair bathroom, kitchen, patio, steps
Chain Link Fencing 751
Chairs
  child's lawn 132,754
  dollhouse 753
  interior 92,306
  lawn 32/39,55/56,169,311,322R, 548,754
  repair,refinish,reupholster 623
Chaise 78,169,312,754
Chalk Line 613,632,668,679,684,685,
Charts, reference
  alarm accessories 695
  aluminum binder bars and carpet grippers 683
  brackets and fasteners 623,761
  carpentry tip 672
  ceiling fixture and lamp repair 694
  concrete block 617,632,697
  drill bits 761
  essentials of brick construction 617,668
  fireplace 674
  glue 623
  kitchen equipment template 608, 658
  layout grid 615,658,684,685
  lumber chart 605,607,609,611
  metric conversion chart 605,606
  plant guide 611
  plumbing charts 675
    beveled cone and slip joint washers, brass friction rings, cap thread, copper and cast iron fittings, dome and square stem bonnet packing, faucet stems, friction rings, lock rings, "O" rings, plastic fittings, renew seats, top bib gaskets.
  roofing reference guide 696
  screw chart 612,623,679
  siding 696
  storage units 605
  wiring diagram 694
    dollhouse wiring 694,753
Chests
  blanket 37,761,792,962
  storage 672
  tool 76,672
  toy and storage 37,65,962,771
  wardrobe 139,658,771
Chicken House 14
Children's Furniture
  blackboard message center 313 578
  blackboard table 117,771
  bookcases and shelves 18,21,192 664

bookends 102B,756
bulletin board 93,607
bunks and beds 68,87,761,771
desk 18,537,761
dollhouse furniture 753
door stops 756
giraffe clothes tree 34,771
headboard 126
lawn chair 132,754
lamp 98
magazine rack 25,920,761
picture frames 623
playtable 117,771
record and hi-fi cabinets 192,272, 436,612
shoe shine box 45
shoe rack 345
step stool 353,771
storage cabinets 138,605
storage chests 37,65,962,761
telephone shelf 313
toys 771
trainboard 190,672
TV tables 16,925
wall decorations 539,580,581,615, 756
wall shelves 4,6,31,35,159M,576, 756,761
Child's Playhouse 148,649
Chimes, Swedish Door 561,672
Chimney 91,910,674,696,753
  capping, construction 674
  cricket 674,696
  flashing 674,696
  flat roof 674
  dollhouse 753
  housing 674
  masonry 674
  outside installation 763
  prefabricated 632,674,685
  slip section 674
China Cabinet, dollhouse 753
Christmas Displays
  angel 769
  angel banner 670
  camels 410C
  candy cane 435
  carolers 331
  choir boys 562
  fireplace mantel 768
  giant outdoor cards, murals 149, 331, 540, 560, 562, 592, 769, 942A, 942B
  illuminated 560,562,592,694,767, 769
  indoor decorations 310,767,768
  madonna 149,540,767
  nativity
    table top 310, life size 410

noel greeting 531
reindeer & sleigh 433,434
santa 431,575
window painting 149
wiring 694
wise men greeting 560
wreath 676
Circuit Breakers 694
Cistern, how to build 617
Clamps 623,754,761
Clapboard Siding 603,609,613,632,
    649,663,684,696,763
Climbing Gym 153
Climbing Pole 154
Closets 605
    under stair 615,773
closet Flanges, pip 675,682
Clothes Tree 34,771
Clothing Storage 605
Cobbler's Bench 102A,586,756,761
    dollhouse size 753
Coffee Tables, see tables
Cold Water Pipes 675,682,685
Collar Beams 679
Collars
    fireplace 674
    smokepipe 674
Columns
    colonial dollhouse 753
    concrete 631,697,781
    jack post 613,615,674,685
    steel 632,697
Colonial
    bed 68,753,761
    bench 23,753,761
    blanket chest 761,962
    bookcase 18,753,761
    cabinet 753,761
    Cape Cod house 514
    candleholder 559
    china cabinet 753,761
    cobbler's bench 102A,586,753,
        756,761
    corner cupboard 38,753
    cradle rocker 753,761
    cupola 609,679,680
    doll cradle 753
    dollhouse furniture 753
    fireplace mantel 605,674,753
    furniture 753,761
    hutch cabinet 270,753,761
    planters 102A,753,756,761,933
    Porsmouth magazine stand 761
    rope spring bed 68,753,761
    step stool 753,771
    table-bench 94,761
    tavern bar 612
    wall shelves 2,24,753,756,761
    weathervane 524

window valance 1,27,30,157,605
Component Systems, stereo 612
Concrete & Masonry 617,668,697
    barbecue 316,668,674
    block chart 617,632
    block layout stick 617
    chimney 674
    colors 617
    culverts, curbs 732,751,679,680
    decorator blocks 582,617
    floors, garage and basement,
        barns 273,606,613,615,617,632,
    footprint stepping stones 96
    foundations and footings 84,86,
        113,609,611,613,617,632,649
    kennel run 751
    mixing 617,697
    patio floor 591,606,617,631,781
    piles 567,617,631,697,781
    repairs 617
    steps 617,685
    story pole 697
    tools 617,697
    tree bench and repair 617
    waterproofing 615,617,663,685,
    work simplified 617
Contemporary Furniture 658
    bars 508,690,718
    bookcases 664
    cabinet furniture 658
    chairs 92,306,311,548
    desk 542
    dining buffet 138,718
    magazine, book rack 658
    planter 82
    record cabinet 192,436,664
    room divider 128,658
    studio bed 623,633
    tables 95,137,140,141,309,452,554
    wardrobe 139,658
Cooler, Attic Air 135
Coping Saw 634,664,753,754,756,
    761
Copper Fittings 675,682
Corner Cabinet 38
Corner Pole 668
Cornice
    how to build 605,612
    install traverse rod 605
Corrugated Ties 663,668,763
Cot, String Bed 68,623,753,761
Cottages, see Homes
Counter 80,243
    sink 606,608,658,685
    tops 608,658,685
Couplings, pipe 675,682,685
Cove Molding
    base 603,605,608,615,658,664,
        665,685,753

ceiling 603,605,658,664,665,674, 753,761
Covering
pipe, girder 605,608,615
ducts 685
Cradles
baby 761
cigarette and match 756
dollhouse 753
Cricket, fireplace 674,696
Cupola, Colonial 609,679,680
Curtain Rods 605

Dado Sets 761
Damper, fireplace 674
Daybed 623,633
Deck 631,763,773,781
Decorations
garden 304,756
lawn 81,96,438,587,607,756,801
patio 582
table 17,43
wall 539, 580, 581, 582, 615, 701, 702, 704, 705, 706, 709, 712, 713, 756, 761
Depth Gauges 607,677,761
Desks 18,139,537,543,658,761
Detectors
fire , smoke 674
Diagonal Bracing 609,613,632,679, 680,697
Dimmer Switches 694
Dining
bench 307
buffet 138,718
table 94,95,137,554,761
Dish Storage 38,246,270,608,658,685
Displays, see Christmas Displays
case 159M,605,607,627,792
Diverter Valve 675,682
Dividers
room 128,308,608,658,792,930
outdoor privacy 582,607,617,631, 668,781,937
Dog Houses 28,751
Doll Carriage 59,61,753
clear enclosure 792
cradle 753,761
display cabinet 792
Dollhouses
open back colonial , packaway
southern colonial 753
Dollhouse Furnituure 753
china cabinet, cobbler's bench, corner cupboard, cradle, dining and occasional chairs, drop leaf table, fireside bench, hutch cabinet, montpelier bookcase,planter, rope spring bed, shaker hutch,

step stool, valance board
Door
alarm 695
bar holder 679
bi-fold 605
bumper 679
canopy 305,607
chimes 561,672,677
decorate with plysculpture 615, 704
dutch door 632,649,679
furnace room door 763
garage 86,663,763
glass sliding 613,695,763,781
hayloft 679
how to install 608,609,613,615,631
provincial trim 623
remove 608,680,684
outside entry 611,615,632,684,754
sliding 605,634,658,679,680,754
stall 679,680
storage 605,672
toolhouse 649
trolley door hanger 679
Dormer, how to build 773
Double Hung Windows 608,609,613, 684,685,763,773
Downspouts, guttering 613,632,679,
Drain 675,682
Drainage Tile 615,617
Drapery
traverse track installation 605
Drawers
how to build 608,612,658,672,677, storage 605,634
Drills 606,615,677,682,694,695,753, 756,761
Drive Pins 612
Driveway
culverts, curbs 732
markers 438,587
Drop Leaf Table, dollhouse 753
Dry Well 609,615,617,632
Ducts, fireplace 674
Dutch Door 679,680

Easel, artists 555
Edging Tool
concrete 617,668
Elbows
fireplace 674
plumbing 675,682
Electric Light Gardening 611,694
Electrical Alarms 695
built-in lighting 694
dollhouse lighting 694,753
repairs, wiring 694
Emergency Power 694
End Tables 99,127,141,925

INDEX TO MONEY-SAVING REPAIRS, IMPROVEMENTS, PATTERNS AND BOOKS

Enclosures, see Built-In, cabinets
books 612,664
brooms, mops 156,634,672
chimney 674
hi-fi and record 192,272,436,612
lavatory 158,606
lighting 694
porch 613,781
pots and pans 578
radiator 672,677
refrigerator 608,658
sink 41,158
trains 190,672,677
truck body camper 594
wall oven 606,658,685
window, see valance 605
Entry, outdoors 611,615,617,632,
Escutcheon 675,682
Excavating 84,86,113,609,611,613,
Expansion Joint 613,617,696,697
Expansion Plug 609,613,615,631,
Express Wagon 40
Exterior Siding 603,609,613,649,663

Fan, window 135
Farmyard Animals 79,756,771
Fascia 609,613,632,663,680,684,696
Fasteners, hollow wall 612
Faucet
repairs, replacement, seat,
stems 675
Feeders, bird 9,669
Fences 607,631,668,781
chain link 751
board 697,941
privacy 607,631,668,781,937
Williamsburg 315,607
Ferrule 675,682
Fiber Glass
bathtub 682,685
insulation 609
membrane 696
panels 611,631,696
Fire Alarms 695
Firebrick 674
Fireplace 73,316,668,674
Christmas 768
fixtures 674
mantel 231,605,674,753
masonry 674
outdoor 316,668
prefabricated 674,685
radiant heat 674
Fisherman's Cabinet 266,630
Fixtures
dollhouse 753
electrical 694,695
plumbing 675,682,685
Flanges, pipe 675,682,685

Flashing
chimney 674,696
dormer 773
skylight 696
roof 609,613,632,649,674,680,696
Flexible Shower 675,682
Float, cartop swimming 247
Floating, concrete 613,617,781
Floodlights 632,694,695
Floor
asphalt vinyl tile 615
carpets 683
ceramic 606
how to lay 615,665,683,685
level 608,685
repair 608,685
underlay 615,683
Flue Pipe 674
Fluorescent
lighting 615,694
lights, plant growing 611,694
Flush Valve, toilet 675
Foam Rubber, upholstery 623
Folding
chair 56
lawn bench 325
picnic table 754
screen 56
settee 55
snack table 43
table 26
Footings 84,86,113,609,611,613,617
Footprints, stepping stone 96
Form, concrete 613,617,668,697
Foundations 84,113,609,611,613,
waterproofing 615,617,632,685,
Frames
picture 623
window 605
Framing 632,697,763
Free Standing
bookcase 612
fireplace 674
room divider 658
Furniture
bars 690
colonial 761
contemporary 658
dollhouse 753
Furniture, repair 623
antiquing 623,761
cane webbing, spring replacement,
refinishing, reupholster 623
Furring 605,609,615,632,685,696,
Fuses
wiring 694

Gable Roof, studs 609,611,632,649, 663,679,680,696,697
Gambrel Rafter Roof 679,697
Garage
  carport 680
  door alarm 695
  doors 86,663,763
  one car 680
  transform into housing 663,763, 684
  transform into stable 680
  two car 663
  two car with apartment above 763
Garden
  greenhouse 611,615
  electric light 611,694
  hotbed 611
  tool house 51,89,649,679
  trellis 304,607
Garment Storage 605
Gaskets, plumbing 675,682
Gates 315,607,941
Gauges, depth 607,677,761
Girders, enclosing 605,615
Glass Sliding Doors 613,695,763,781
Glazing 603,609,613,623,684,685, 773,781
Glider, lawn 754
Gluing, complete guide 623
  furniture 623,753,761
Gol Cart 583
Grade Level Establishing 609,611, 613,617,632,663,697,763
Grain Box 679
Grates, fireplace 674
Greenhouses
  walk in 611
  window 566
Grout
  tile 606
  concrete 613,617,668,781
Guest House 84,684,763
Guide Lines, laying out 84,86,113,
Guides, drilling 677,761
Gun
  cabinet 266,630
  racks 630
Gutters 609,613,632,679,684,696,
Gymnasium, outdoor 152,153,154

Half Lap Joints 761
Hammer, electric jack 680,685,697
Hamster Cage 751
Handles
  barn door 680
Hangers
  barn door 679,680
Hardware
  drapery 605

garage door 86
Harness, roofing safety 696
Hauling Cart 66,679
Headboard 126
Header, framing 632,680,697
Head, shower 675,682
Hearth
  installation 674
  prefabricated 674
Heat, radiant fireplace 674
Heating
  hot air 685
Hi-fi Cabinet 276,612
Hinges
  continuous 753
  door 679,680
  gate 607
Hobby Horse 54,71
Hobby Tables, workbenches 672
Hog House 13
Hole Cutter 606
Hole Digger 607
Homes
  country cottage 91
  five-bedroom Cape Cod 514
  garage 663,680,684,763
  guesthouse 84
  hillside 103H (plans only)
  southwest corner 432,632
  three-bedroom modern 502,513
  three-bedroom ranch 501
  two-bedroom ranch 910
  valley house 103V (plans only)
Home Workshop 672
Hood, hearth 674
Hot Air Circulating Fireplace 674
Hotbed, garden 611
Hot Plate Repair 694
Houseboat 26' - 676
  pontoons 600
House Numbers, signs 607,801
Houses
  bird 669
  dog 28,751
  chicken 14
  doll 753
  duck-inn 751,725
  garden tool 51,89,649,679
  greenhouse 611,615
  lean-to storage 89,649,751
  martin 669
  play 148,649
  rahabilitate 685
  retirement 632
  wiring 694
Hunter's Cabinet 266,630
Hutch
  cabinet 270,761
  dollhouse 753

INDEX TO MONEY-SAVING REPAIRS, IMPROVEMENTS, PATTERNS AND BOOKS

rabbit 751
Hydrant Installation 679,680
Hydraulic Jack 680,684

Increaser 675,682
Indirect Lighting 694
Insulation 609,613,632,697
Iron Pipes 682
Iron Railings, repair 617,685

Jack Hammer 680,685,697
Jack Posts 613,615,674,685
Jamb 605,697
Jewelers Saw 753
Jig Saw Pattern Asst. 102A
 17 full size patterns 756
Jig, rafter 679,680
Jointers 617,668
Joist Hangers 609

Kayak 317,757
Kayfer Fitting 675,682
Kitchen
 blackboard 578
 broom closet 156,634,672
 buffet 138
 cabinets 243,244,245,246,605,608
  634,658,685
 counters 80,243,244,245,605,608
 equipment templates 608,658
 floors 608,685
 knife rack 8
 lighting 694
 modernizing 608,658,685
 planning 608,632,658,685
 range installation 608,685
 refrigerator modernization 605
 serving counter 80,243
 sink enclosure 80,243
 sink trap 682
 sink enclosure 41,158,606
 sink trap 682
 traverse track 605
 utility closet 156
 wall shelves 2,4,5,8
 wall oven 608,685
 workbench 573
Kite, Bermuda 314,771
Knick-Knack, see shelves

Ladder Tie 668
Lamps
 modern table 98
 outdoor colonial post 607,935
 planter 541
 repair 694
 rooster pin up 533
 shadow box 301,557
Lamptable 99,127,141,925

Latches
 door 680
 gate 607
Lavatory Enclosure 158,606
 P trap 675,682
 repair 675
Lawn, Patio
 bench 57,307,325,754
 chairs 32/39,55/56,311,322R,548
 chaise 78,169,312,754
 fenches 607,631,668,781
 furniture repairs 623
 glider 754
 ornaments 9,81,96,102A,756
 settee 55/56,754
 tables 17,22,75,322R,554,577,754
Layout Stick
 bricklaying 668,674
 concrete 617,697
 clapboard siding 609,763,781
 tile 606
Lazy Susan 608,672,677
Lead Sealants, pipe 682
Lean-to Tool Shed 89,649
 kennel 751
Letter Boxes 607
Level-Transit 668,697,763
Lighting 694
 built-in cornice, valance 605,694
 dark corner 557
 luminous ceiling 615,694
 outdoor 632,694,695,763
 wall sconce, candle 559
 walls, soffits, cove 694
Line Holder 668
Lintel, fireplace 674
Lock, alarm 695
Lounge, chaise 78,169,312,754
Louver
 how to install 632,665,679,763,773
Magazine Rack 25,658,761,920
Magnetic Catch 605
Magnetic Contact Alarms 695
Mailbox, roadside 607
Mantel
 fireplace 231,605,674,753
 dollhouse 753
Martin House 669
Masonry, cement 668
Masonry Drill 615,680
Masonry Fireplace 674
Medicine Chest, repair 694
Message Center,blackboard313,578
Metal Clips 668
Metal Repairs, roofing 696
Meter, multitester 694
Modern Furniture 658
 see furniture, bookcase, table

Modernization
attic 773
bathroom 606,682,685
basement 605,615
kitchen 608,658,685
lighting 694
metal and wood cabinets 605, 608,685
refrigerator 605,608,685
Mortar, how to mix 617,668,685
apply 609,613,617,668,685
Mortising 607,664,761
Music Wall 612

Name Plates, signs 438,587,607,801
Nailing Machine 605
Night Tables 343

Oriental Plysculpture 704,712
Ornamental Ironwork 617
Ornaments, see Decorations
see Christmas 694
door chimes 561,672,677
driveway 438
lawn 9,81,96,102A,617,631,756
sign & nameplate 607,756
table top 46
wall hanging 301,539,559
Outbuildings, see Houses
Outdoor Furniture, how to build 754
bench, chair, chaise, glider, picnic table, table
Outdoor Lighting 694
Outlets, electrical 694
Ovens, built-in 608,658,685
Overhead Garage Door 86,663,763

Panels
aluminum roofing 679,696,684
ceiling 609,613,615,665,684,685,
circuit breaker 694,695
fiber glass 611,631,696
plexiglas 792
Paneling, how to apply 605
Paneling Arches 605
Parakeet Cage 751
Parging, also pargeting 617,668
Parquet, flooring 685
Partitions 609,613,615, 632,658
dollhouse 753
stable 679,680
Patio
decorations, see ornaments
furniture, see lawn
how to build 606,617,631,668,781
how to screen 631,781
lighting 694
paver tile 606,617,631,781

Peasant Bench 57
shelf 2,4
Perimeter Alarm System 695
Pet Projects 751
cat shelter, cavy cage, dog house, kennel and run, duck house, hamster, parakeet cage, rabbit hutch
Photo Electric System 695
Picnic
benches 22,57,325,754
tables 22,554,577,754
Picture Frames 623
Pier, concrete 607,609,668,763
Pilaster 664,668
Pin-up Lamp 533
Pipe Rack 49,630
Pipes
cast iron 682,675
chimney 674
drain 611,675,679,680,682
enclosure 605,615
galvanized 611,682
kitchen 675,682
lavatory 606,675,682
plastic 675,679,682
repair 675
smokepipe 674
Pipe Scaffold 668,674,763
Planters
dollhouse 753
indoor 46,82,102A,756,761,933
lamp 541
Plant Box Rack 611
Plaques, child's wall 102A,756
Plastic Laminate
how to apply 608,658,685
Plastic Panels 611,631,696
Platforms
stairway 603,615,617,632,665,773
raised platform for hearth 674
Playground Equipment 20,63,152, 153,154
Playhouses 148,649
Playroom Bar 612,690
Playroom Furniture
blackboard playtable 117, 771
giraffe clothes tree 34,771
tot's step stool & TV chair 353,771
toy chest on wheels 65,771
Plumb, how to 609,611,613,615
Plumbing
bathtub installation 682
cast iron fittings 675,682
charts, closet bends, continuous waste, copper fitting, diverter valve, drain, drum trap, faucet, ferrule, fiber glass bathtub, fittings, fixtures, framing, fresh air

inlet, glossary, gypsum board application, horizontal branch, increaser, kayfer fittings, kitchen faucet replacement, kitchen sink trap, lavatory, lavatory faucet replacement, lavatory installation, lock ring, O-ring, pipes, plastic pipe, plumbing wall, repair, replace toilet bowl seal, revent, rough in, septic tank, slip joint, soil pipe, solder cup end, spigot, stack, stack vent, sump pump installation, telephone shower, wall frame, water pipe riser, water tank repair, toilet 675,682,
Plunger, toilet 675,682,685
Polyethylene 609,613,617,663
Plywood, how to panel 605
Pontoon 600,676
Pony
 book ends 102A,756
 rocker 53,771
Porch
 add-on 567,631,781
 build, columns, enclose, screening 613,631,781
 sliding glass doors 613,763,781
Post Driver 751
Post Hole Digger 607
Post, fence 607,781
Potholders, holder 756
Power Tool Workbench 677
Pram
 boat 77
Privacy Partition 607,631,668,781,
Propane Troch 617
Pumps, sump 615,617,675,685

Quarry Tile 606,617

Rabbit Hutch 751
Racks
 can storage 634,672
 cassette tape 612
 clothes 605
 gun 630
 magazine 25,761,920
 pipe, smoking 49,630
 shoe 345
 storage 605,634
 tool 672
 towel 29
Radar Alarm 695
Radial Arm Saw
 workbench 677
Radiator Enclosure 672
Radio and Stereo
 bar 690
 cabinets 272,612
 how to build-in 612

Rafters 609,611,631,632,663,679,
Rail Fencing 607,781,941
Railings, iron 617,685
Rain Cap, chimney 674
Range Installation 608,658,685
Razor Saw 753
Record Cabinet 192,436,658,664,690
Record Changer, recorders, tapes 612
Recreation Room 615
 furniture, bar 612,690
 how to modernize a basement 615
 lighting 694
Rectangular Tie 668
Reducers, pipe 675,682
Refinishing Furniture 623,761
Refrigerator
 enclosure 608,658,685
 modernizing 605,608,685
Reinforcing Rods, wire 617,668,697
Reinforced Masonry 668
Relax-a-board 161
Relief Valves, plumbing 675,682
Remodeling 609,685,781
Remote Detector Alarm 695
 switch 695
Repair
 basement walls 615,617,685
 cane webbing 623
 concrete,masonry 617,668
 electrical 694
 furniture 623
 picture frame 623
 plumbing 675
 roofing 696
 tile 606
 window sash 685
Retaining Walls 668
Revolving Tool Turret 672
Reupholstery 623
Ridge Caps
 roofing 696
 shingles 696
Rifle Cabinets and Racks 630
Rings
 drapery 605
 plumbing 675
Rip Saws 613,664,677,754,761
Roadside Mailbox Rack 607
Roadside Sign 607
Rocker
 colonial crib 761
 dollhouse cradle 753
 pony ride 53,771
Rod
 reinforcing 617,668,697
 ties 697
 traverse 627
Roll Roofing 696

Roller
barn door 679,680
garage door 86,680,684
Roofing Repairs
and application
asphalt, built-up, metal, wood,
slate, asphalt shingles, roll roofing, 696
chimney cricket 674,696
dollhouse 753
flashing 603,609,696
heating cable, tape 694
metal 696
safety harness, scaffold 696
vent 674,675,679,696
Room, add on 609,760,773
attic 773
basement 615
bathroom 609,682,685,773
dividers 128,308,608,658,930
Rope, safety harness 696
Routers 608,697,753,761
Rowboats 77,85
Rug 683
adhesive, tape, backing, binder
bars, grippers, padding, seaming,
under carpet alarm 683,695
Rush Weaving 623

Saber Saw 674,677,685,753,754,
756,761
Saber Saw Patterns 102A,756
Safety
alarms 695
harness 696
relief valves 675,682,685
signs 438,587
switches, electric 694
Sailboat 194,248
Sandbox 20,77
Sanitary Tee 682
Sash, window
alarm 695
cellar 663,679
repair 685
steel 603,609,613
Sawhorse Toolchest 672
Sconce, candle wall 559
Screed 617,631,663
Screen Enclosure 613,631,781
Screen, folding 706,712
Screw Chart 612,623
Scribing 605,609
Scroll Saw
patterns 756
Sealing Cord 631,781
Seaming Tape, carpet 683
Sectional Bookcase 664

Security Devices 695
auto, fire, door, garage door, fire
sensors, under carpet, window
Service Center 243
counter 80
Settee, lawn 39,55,754
Sewer Line 675,682,685
Sewer Rod 675
Sewing Cabinet 634,672
table 543
Shadow Box 301,557
Shaker Hutch Table 94,761
dollhouse furniture 753
Sheathing, exterior 603,609,613
Shelf Standards 664,792
Shelves, wall 2,4,5,6,8,21,24,605
Shingles, asphalt 113,696,910
roofing 432,609,663,696
Shoe Rack 345
Shoe Shine Box 45
Showers and Fittings 675,682,685
Shutoff Valves, plumbing 675,682,
685
Shutters, dollhouse 753
Siding 603,609,613,632,663,684
dollhouse 753
Signs, nameplates 438,587,607,801
Sill Beam 609,632,684,697
Single Handle Faucet 675
Sink
bar 201,608,658,690
bases 158,606,608,675,682
counter installation 606,608,
658,685
enclosure 41,158
faucets, fittings 608,675,682,685
Skylight, how to install 696,773
Slab Construction 680
Slant Board 161
Slate Roofing 696
Slide, child's 63
Sliding Door, wardrobes 139,658
Sliding Stable Door 679,680
Smokepipe, adapter elbow 674
Smoke Detector 695
Snake, sewer 675
Snips, aviation 674
Soffit 603,605
Soil Pipe 682
Solder Ring 695
Sound Amplifier 612
Speakers
intercom 695
radio, stereo, tape 612
Speakers 612
Spindle 675
Sportsman Revolving Cabinet 630
Springs, furniture, cord bed 623,761
retying, replacing, no-sag 623

INDEX TO MONEY-SAVING REPAIRS, IMPROVEMENTS, PATTERNS AND BOOKS

Stable 679,680
Stacking Tables 43
Stair Carriage 615,632,697,763,773
Stairs, concrete 613,615,617,631
  concrete repair 685
  how to build 615,617,632,763
Stall Door 679,680
Stands
  drill 677
  mailbox 607
  radial arm saw 677
  television 925
Starter Tee 674
Steel Girder Bridging 632
Steps 603,613,615,617,632,685
Step Flashing 603,609,696,773
Stereo Wall 612
Stilts 552,771
Stool, sill 605,609,613,632
Stool, tot's step 353,771
Storage 605
  cabinets, see cabinets 672
  canned goods 608,770
  chest 37,65,672,761,962
  doll 159M,605,679,792
  garden tool house, lean-to 89,649
  headboard 126
  room divider 128,308,608,658
  sewing 543,634,672
  tool 672
  trainboard 672
  underbed 37
  undersink 41,158,606
  understair 605,615,773
  walls 190.605,612,658
  wine storage 690
Storm Collar 674
Storm Windows 303,792
Story Pole 668,674
Stringer, stair 603,615,632,665,697
Structural Lighting 694
Studio Bed, string 633,623,761
Studs 84,91,501,502,609,697
Subflooring 603,606,632,763,773
Sump Pump 615,617,675,685
Sundeck 631,763,773,781
Sunhouse 611
Surfboard or Swimming Float 247
Suspended Ceiling 609,613,615
Swimming Pool Enclosure 631,781
Swings 152,754
Switch Lock 695
Switch, wall 605,694

"T" Hinge 679,680
Tables
  bar 140,690
  bench 672
  bridge 95
  child's 117
  coffee 52,140,309,326,452
  colonial 94,761
  dining 94,95,137,554
  end 99,127,141
  folding 94,961
  lawn or terrace 17,75,326,554
  picnic 17,22,577
  roundtop 75,326
  serving, see coffee
  sewing 543
  TV 16,923
  wall, attached 26,774
  workshop 568,573,672
Tape Recorder, built in 612
Teenuts 672
Telephone
  dialer alarm 695
  shower 675
Termite Shield 609,632,763,697
Terrace 631,668,781
  table 75,326
Tile, see Ceramic 606
  asphalt 615
  counter 606
  how to lay 606,615
  patio design 617
  vinyl 615
Toilet
  installation 682
  repairs,replacement 675
Tool Chest 71,672
Tommy Gun, see toys
Tool Houses
  garage 113,680
  garden 649
  lean-to 89,649
  red barn 679
Tote Box 677
Tourist House 84,684
Towel Rack 29
Toys
  airplane 70
  animals 79,83,771
  artists easel 555
  boats 60,67,771
  carriage 59,771
  chest 771
  circus group 48,771
  climbing, see playground
  clown 47,771
  dollhouses 753
  furniture, see Children's
  gas cart 583
  glider 70
  gym, see playground
  hobby horse 54,771
  machine gun 62
  playground equipment

climbing pole 154
complete gym 152
merry-go-round 733
monkey bar 153
sandbox 20,77
slide 63
playhouse 148,649
playtable 117,771
pony rocker 53,771
stable 679
step stool 353,771
stilts 552,771
storage 65,605,771
toychest 65,771
wagon 40
wheelbarrow 66
workbench 15,672
Trainboard 190,677
Transformer 694,695,753
Trap 675,682
    bathtub, drum, lavatory, sink,
    waste line
Traverse Track 605
Tree Well 668
Trellis 305,607,631
Trim
    apply 615
    charts 623,664
Trolley Door Hanger, Rail,
    Bracket 679
Trophy Cabinet 630,792
Truss Rafter 697
Tub Sets 606,682,685
Tungsten Carbide Tip Drills 615,674
Turntable 612
TV Table 16
    bar 690
Two Handle Faucets 675

Ultrasonic Alarm 695
Under Bed Storage 761,792
Under Stair Storage 615
Upholstery, repair 623
Utility Closet 156,634

Valance
    bookcase 271
    indirect lighting 157,694
    window 1,27,30,550,627
Valley Flashing 696
Vanity 658
    bathroom 606
Veneer, brick 668

Wall Decorations 97,159M,539,580,
    581,702, see ornaments
Wall
    cabinets 658
    framing 663,663,684,763

gypsum board 605,763,773
oven 608,658,685
paneling 605
plaque, child's 102A
remove 608,685
retaining 668
shelves, see shelves
storage 605
switch 605,694
waterproof 615,617
wiring 694
walks,brick 668
Wardrobe 139,193,263,605,658
Washers
    faucet 675
Water Pipe Riser 682
Water Shut Off
    valve 675
Waterproofing 617
    cement 617,632,697
Wattage Chart 694,763
Weathervane 524,588
Webbing, furniture 623
Wheelbarrow 66
Windbraces 632,680
Window
    bookcase 271
    bow, picture, installation 609
    framing 159
    glazing 613,623,773,781
    greenhouse 566,611
    guards 679
    how to install 609,613,679,781
    how to move 608
    how to repair window 685,773
    how to replace window 773
    storm 303,792
    valance 1,27,30,550,605
Wire Clips 623,773,685
Wire Hangers 617
Wireless Alarm, Intercom Unit 695
Wiring, electric 694
Wood Conversion Chart 613
Wood Shingles 696
Workbench 568,672
Workshop 672
Worktable 573,672
Wren House 11,111,669,756

"Z" Tie 668

Guides To Good Living

*FULL SIZE PATTERNS INCLUDED

603 — How to Build a Dormer — 82pp. 114 illus.
605 —* How to Install Paneling, Build Valances, Cornices, Wall to Wall
Storage, Cedar Room, Fireplace Mantel — 146pp. 214 illus.
606 — How to Lay Ceramic Tile — 98pp. 137 illus.
607 — How to Build Fences,Gates,Outdoor Projects—162pp. 212 illus.
608 — How to Modernize a Kitchen—82pp. 118 illus.
609 — How to Build an Addition—162pp. 211 illus.
611 — How to Build Greenhouses - Sunhouses—114pp. 110 illus.
612 — How to Build Wall-to-Wall Cabinets,
Stereo Installation Simplified—130pp. 165 illus.
613 — How to Build or Enclose a Porch—82pp. 112 illus.
615 — How to Modernize a Basement—98pp. 135 illus.
617 — Concrete Work Simplified—130pp. 193 illus.
623 — How to Repair,Refinish&ReupholsterFurniture—98pp.138illus.
630 — How to Build Sportsman's Revolving Storage
Cabinet—98pp. 121 illus.
631 — How to Build Patios & Sundecks—98pp. 133 illus.
632 — How to Build a Vacation or Retirement House—194pp.170 illus.
634 — How to Build Storage Units—98pp. 145 illus.
649 — How to Build a Garden Tool House,
Child's Playhouse—82pp. 107 illus.
658 — How to Build Kitchen Cabinets, Room Dividers
and Cabinet Furniture—98pp. 134 illus.
663 — How to Build a Two Car Garage, Lean-To Porch,
Cabana—130pp. 142 illus.
664 — How to Construct Built-In and Sectional Bookcases—
98pp. 137 illus.
665 — How to Modernize an Attic—82pp. 86 illus.
668 — Bricklaying Simplified—146pp. 212illus.
669 — How to Build Birdhouses & Bird Feeders—66pp. 86 illus.
672 —* How to Build Workbenches, Tool Chests—180pp. 250 illus.

* Read * Learn * Save *

other Easi-Bild books

674 — How to Install a Fireplace—242pp. 354 illus.

675 — Plumbing Repairs Simplified—194pp. 820 illus.

677 — How to Build a Home Workshop—98pp. 133 illus.

679 — How to Build a Stable
      & Red Barn Tool House—178pp. 197 illus.

680 — How to Build a One Car Garage, Carport,
      Convert a Garage into a Stable—146pp. 181 illus.

682 — How to Add an Extra Bathroom—162pp. 200 illus.

683 — Carpeting Simplified—146pp. 212 illus.

684 — How to Transform a Garage into Living Space—130pp. 139 illus.

685 — How to Remodel Buildings—258pp. 345 illus.

690 — How to Build Bars—162pp. 195 illus.

694 — Electrical Repairs Simplified,
      Dollhouse Wiring—134pp. 218 illus.

695 — How to Install Protective Alarm Devices—130pp. 146 illus.

696 — Roofing Simplified—130pp. 168 illus.

697 — Forms, Footings, Foundations, Framing,
      Stair Building—210pp. 308 illus.

751 — How to Build Pet Housing—178pp. 252 illus.

753 — How to Build Dollhouses & Furniture—194pp. 316 illus.

754 —* How to Build Outdoor Furniture—130pp. 174 illus.

756 — Scroll Saw Projects—130pp. 146 illus.

757 —* How to Build a Kayak - 14'3'', 16'9'', 18'0''—66pp., plus pattern

761 — How to Build Colonial Furniture—258pp. 342 illus.

763 —* How to Build a Two Car Garage
      with Apartment Above—194pp. 226 illus.

771 —* Toymaking & Children's Furniture Simplified—194pp. 330 illus.

773 — How to Create Room at the Top—162pp. 239 illus.

781 — How to Build a Patio, Porch & Sundeck—146pp. 220 illus.

600 — Complete Catalog — illustrates Patterns and Books
      130pp. 300 illus.

Write to Directions Simplified Inc. P.O Box 215 Briarcliff Manor NY 10510 for complete information concerning Easi-Bild Patterns and Home Improvement Books

HANDY - REFERENCE - LUMBER

PLYWOOD - FLAKEBOARD - HARDBOARD - MOLDINGS

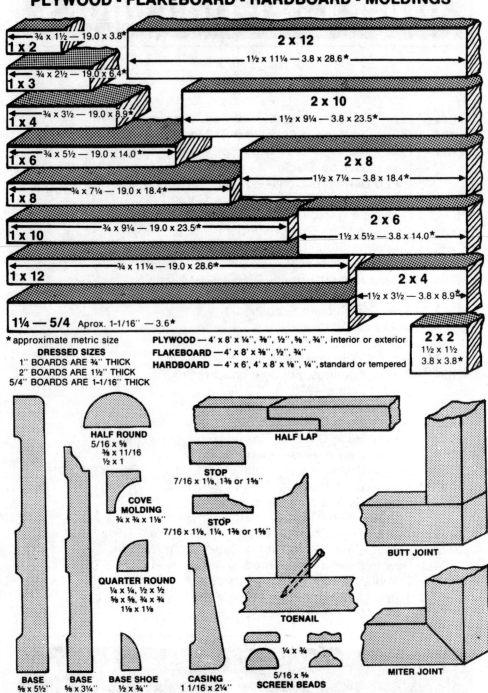

1 x 2 ¾ x 1½ — 19.0 x 3.8*

1 x 3 ¾ x 2½ — 19.0 x 6.4*

1 x 4 ¾ x 3½ — 19.0 x 8.9*

1 x 6 ¾ x 5½ — 19.0 x 14.0*

1 x 8 ¾ x 7¼ — 19.0 x 18.4*

1 x 10 ¾ x 9¼ — 19.0 x 23.5*

1 x 12 ¾ x 11¼ — 19.0 x 28.6*

1¼ — 5/4 Aprox. 1-1/16" — 3.6*

2 x 12 1½ x 11¼ — 3.8 x 28.6*

2 x 10 1½ x 9¼ — 3.8 x 23.5*

2 x 8 1½ x 7¼ — 3.8 x 18.4*

2 x 6 1½ x 5½ — 3.8 x 14.0*

2 x 4 1½ x 3½ — 3.8 x 8.9*

2 x 2 1½ x 1½ / 3.8 x 3.8*

* approximate metric size

DRESSED SIZES
1" BOARDS ARE ¾" THICK
2" BOARDS ARE 1½" THICK
5/4" BOARDS ARE 1-1/16" THICK

PLYWOOD — 4' x 8' x ¼", ⅜", ½", ⅝", ¾", interior or exterior
FLAKEBOARD — 4' x 8' x ⅜", ½", ¾"
HARDBOARD — 4' x 6', 4' x 8' x ⅛", ¼", standard or tempered

HALF ROUND
5/16 x ⅝
⅜ x 11/16
½ x 1

HALF LAP

COVE MOLDING
¾ x ¾ x 1⅛"

STOP
7/16 x 1⅛, 1⅜ or 1⅝"

STOP
7/16 x 1⅛, 1¼, 1⅜ or 1⅝"

QUARTER ROUND
¼ x ¼, ½ x ½
⅝ x ⅝, ¾ x ¾
1⅛ x 1⅛

TOENAIL

BUTT JOINT

MITER JOINT

BASE
⅝ x 5½"

BASE
⅝ x 3¼"

BASE SHOE
½ x ¾"

CASING
1 1/16 x 2¼"

SCREEN BEADS
¼ x ¾
5/16 x ⅝

HANDY REFERENCE-SCREWS

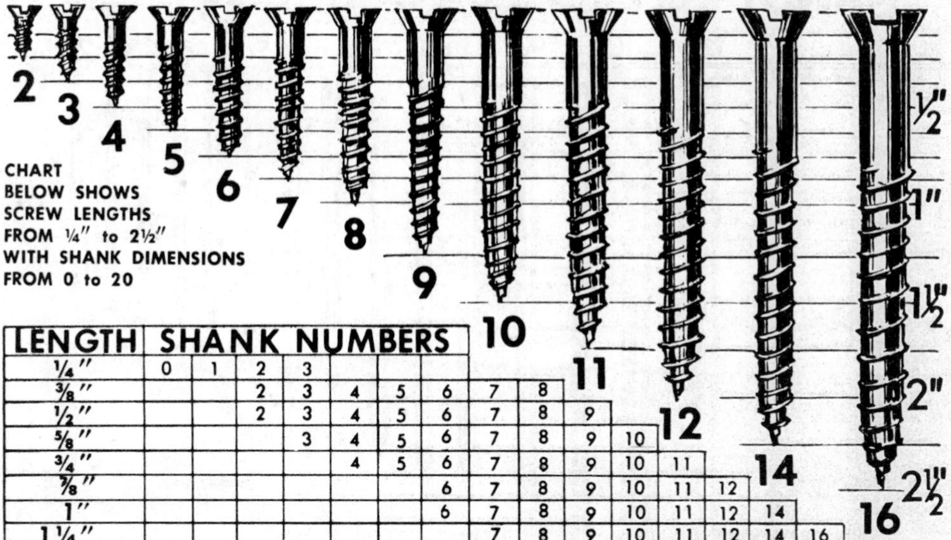
2
3
4
5
6
7
8
9
10
11
12
14
16
1/2"
1"
1 1/2"
2"
2 1/2"

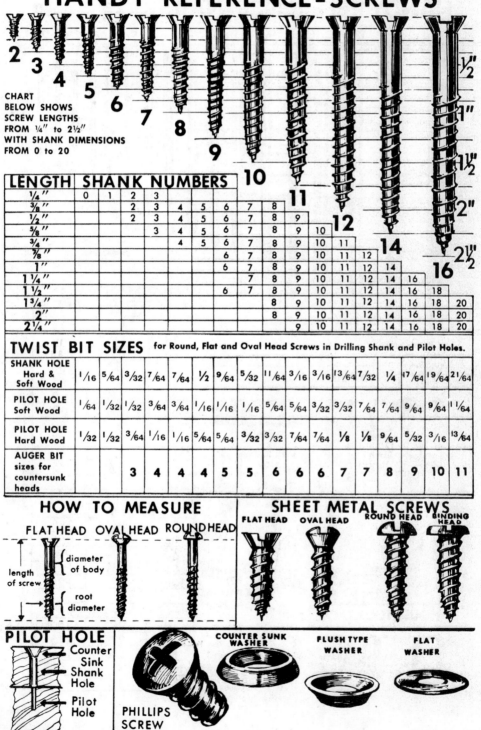

CHART
BELOW SHOWS
SCREW LENGTHS
FROM 1/4" to 2 1/2"
WITH SHANK DIMENSIONS
FROM 0 to 20

LENGTH	SHANK NUMBERS																
1/4"	0	1	2	3													
3/8"			2	3	4	5	6	7	8								
1/2"			2	3	4	5	6	7	8	9							
5/8"				3	4	5	6	7	8	9	10						
3/4"					4	5	6	7	8	9	10	11					
7/8"							6	7	8	9	10	11	12				
1"							6	7	8	9	10	11	12	14			
1 1/4"								7	8	9	10	11	12	14	16		
1 1/2"							6	7	8	9	10	11	12	14	16	18	
1 3/4"									8	9	10	11	12	14	16	18	20
2"									8	9	10	11	12	14	16	18	20
2 1/4"										9	10	11	12	14	16	18	20

TWIST BIT SIZES for Round, Flat and Oval Head Screws in Drilling Shank and Pilot Holes.

SHANK HOLE Hard & Soft Wood	1/16	5/64	3/32	7/64	7/64	1/2	9/64	5/32	11/64	3/16	3/16	13/64	7/32	1/4	17/64	19/64	21/64
PILOT HOLE Soft Wood	1/64	1/32	1/32	3/64	3/64	1/16	1/16	1/16	5/64	5/64	3/32	3/32	7/64	7/64	9/64	9/64	11/64
PILOT HOLE Hard Wood	1/32	1/32	3/64	1/16	1/16	5/64	5/64	3/32	3/32	7/64	7/64	1/8	1/8	9/64	5/32	3/16	13/64
AUGER BIT sizes for countersunk heads			3	4	4	4	5	5	6	6	6	7	7	8	9	10	11

HOW TO MEASURE

FLAT HEAD OVAL HEAD ROUND HEAD

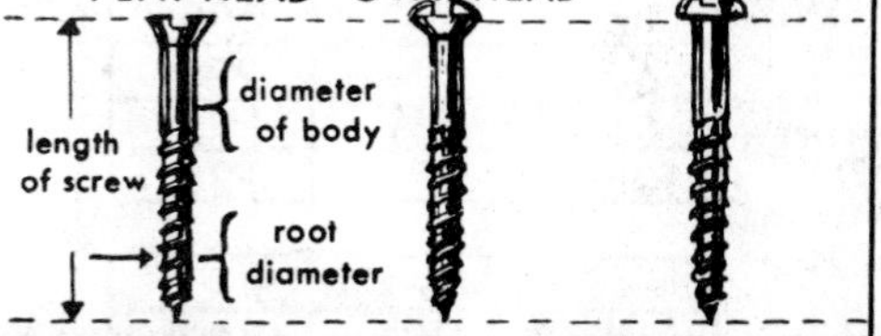
length
of screw
diameter
of body
root
diameter

SHEET METAL SCREWS

FLAT HEAD OVAL HEAD ROUND HEAD BINDING HEAD

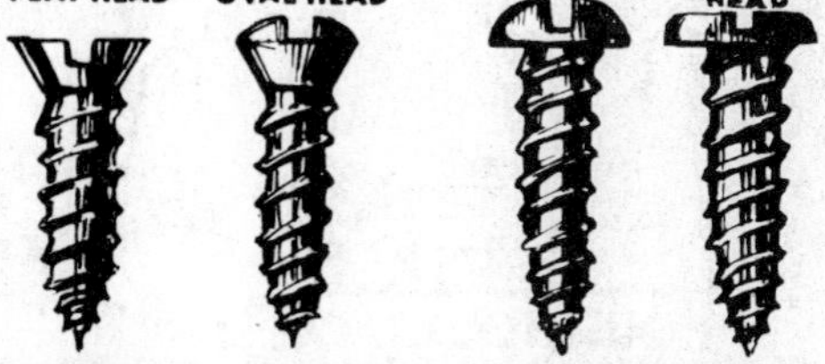

PILOT HOLE

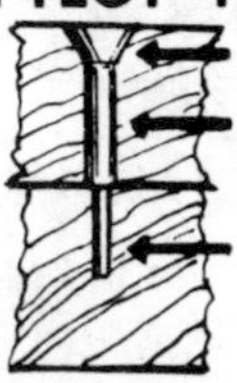
Counter
Sink
Shank
Hole
Pilot
Hole

PHILLIPS
SCREW

COUNTER SUNK WASHER
FLUSH TYPE WASHER
FLAT WASHER

HANDY REFERENCE-NAILS

Common — Finishing —

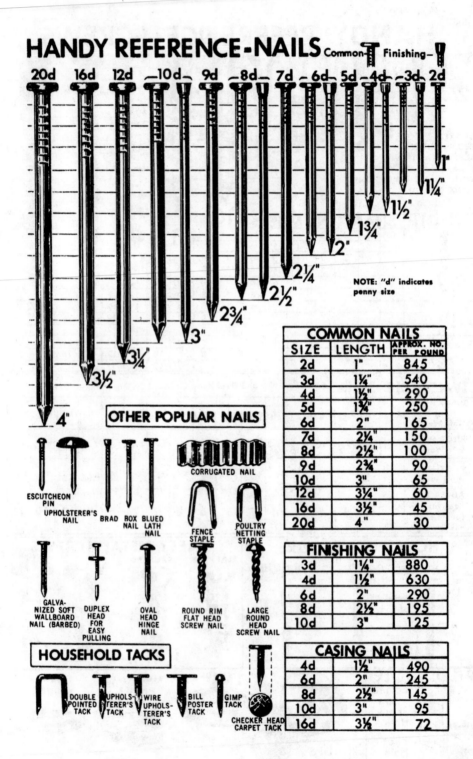

20d 16d 12d 10d 9d 8d 7d 6d 5d 4d 3d 2d

1"

1¼"

1½"

1¾"

2"

2¼"

2½"

2¾"

3"

3¼"

3½"

4"

NOTE: "d" indicates penny size

OTHER POPULAR NAILS

ESCUTCHEON PIN

UPHOLSTERER'S NAIL

BRAD

BOX NAIL

BLUED LATH NAIL

CORRUGATED NAIL

FENCE STAPLE

POULTRY NETTING STAPLE

GALVA-NIZED SOFT WALLBOARD NAIL (BARBED)

DUPLEX HEAD FOR EASY PULLING

OVAL HEAD HINGE NAIL

ROUND RIM FLAT HEAD SCREW NAIL

LARGE ROUND HEAD SCREW NAIL

HOUSEHOLD TACKS

DOUBLE POINTED TACK

UPHOLS-TERER'S TACK

WIRE UPHOLS-TERER'S TACK

BILL POSTER TACK

GIMP TACK

CHECKER HEAD CARPET TACK

COMMON NAILS

SIZE	LENGTH	APPROX. NO. PER POUND
2d	1"	845
3d	1¼"	540
4d	1½"	290
5d	1¾"	250
6d	2"	165
7d	2¼"	150
8d	2½"	100
9d	2¾"	90
10d	3"	65
12d	3¼"	60
16d	3½"	45
20d	4"	30

FINISHING NAILS

3d	1¼"	880
4d	1½"	630
6d	2"	290
8d	2½"	195
10d	3"	125

CASING NAILS

4d	1½"	490
6d	2"	245
8d	2½"	145
10d	3"	95
16d	3½"	72

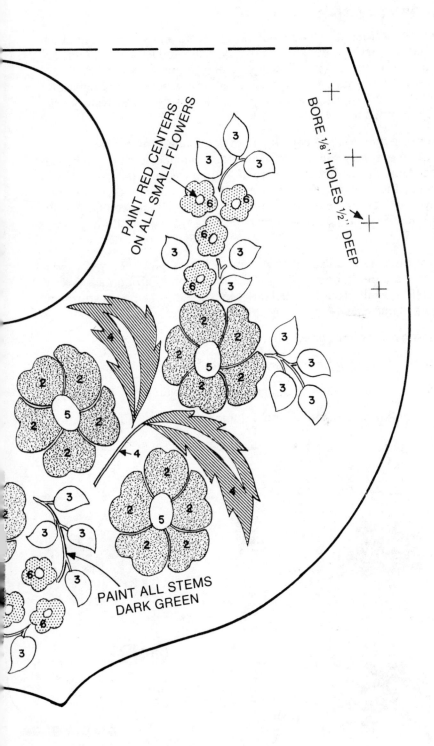

BORE ⅛" HOLES ½" DEEP

PAINT RED CENTERS
ON ALL SMALL FLOWERS

PAINT ALL STEMS
DARK GREEN

179

CARPENTRY TIPS

As every interested individual soon discovers, carpentry is about as difficult to master as cooking, and as complicated as sewing. And like making love, it's something everyone enjoys doing, and learns to do real well, with a little practice. As every home buyer and apartment dweller quickly finds out, what passes for carpentry on one job is considered wood butchery on another.

Buying the right tools, and using them frequently, provides good living at a price everyone can afford. Good tools provide some of life's best companionship. Those who were all thumbs as youngsters, and still consider themselves poor craftsmen, are frequently in for a surprise. Many don't appreciate how time changes one's capabilities. With simplified directions, the author believes anybody can do anything, and do it well.

When you need to drill a number of holes to one depth, it can be done by making a depth gauge, Illus. 226. Drill the hole through a block of wood. Place bit through hole. Mark block the exact amount you want bit to project. Saw block along this line.

Or purchase a depth gauge, Illus. 227.

Another way is to wrap adhesive tape around bit, Illus. 228.

Using a drill stand, Illus. 229, insures drilling plumb holes.

If you don't have a stand, clamp a guide block, Illus. 230, in position.

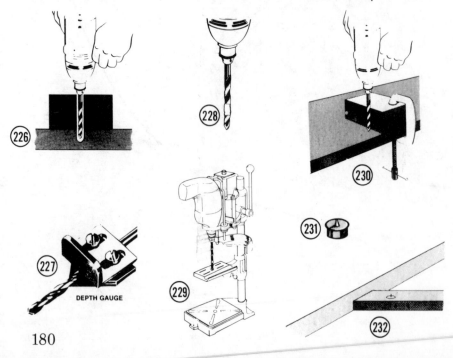

226

228

230

231

227 DEPTH GAUGE

229

232

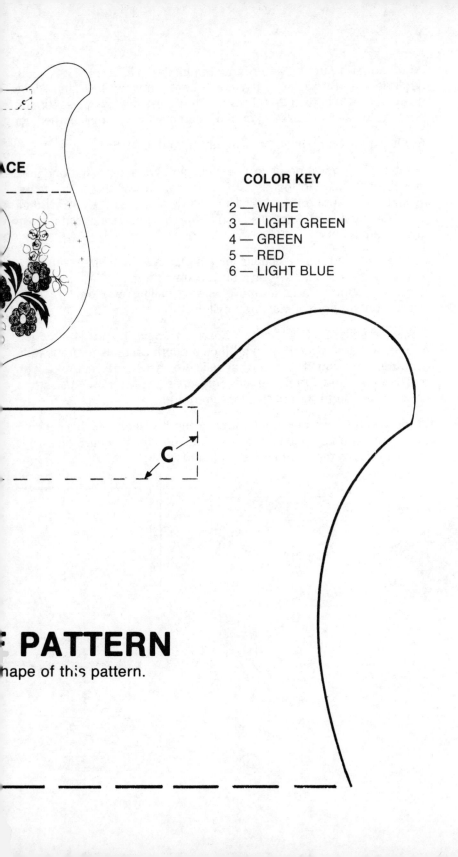

ACE

COLOR KEY

2 — WHITE
3 — LIGHT GREEN
4 — GREEN
5 — RED
6 — LIGHT BLUE

C

PATTERN

hape of this pattern.

When squaring up the end of framing lumber, i.e., 2 x 4, 2 x 6, 2 x 8, beginners find it easier to make a square cut when they draw lines down both edges, Illus. 243. They also find it easier to keep a saw blade perpendicular, Illus. 244, when they clamp a 1 x 2 alongside the line.

A folding measure, Illus. 245, greatly simplifies measuring.

Lumber size shown on page 176 is current. While a 2 x 4 at one time measured a full two inches by four inches, it was, for many years, available measuring 1⅝ x 3⅝". Currently it measures 1½ x 3½". Since a 2 x 4 is most frequently used in framing, the new size doesn't cause any repair problem.

House framing follows established standards. A floor span with 2 x 8 joists spaced 12" apart will be found acceptable up to 13'4" in length, if it doesn't support a lathe and plastered ceiling; and only 12'0" in length if it supports a plastered ceiling.

Codes specify 2 x 8 joists 16" apart on spans up to 11'0" when supporting a plastered ceiling. Since modernization work frequently requires replacing 2 x 8 joists that measure anywhere from a full 2 x 8" to 1⅝ x 7½", and current lumber only measures 1½ x 7¼", use strips of ¼" plywood to fur out thickness required.

When you butt one piece of lumber to another, Illus. 246, it's called a butt joint. When you cut lumber to 45°, using a miter square, Illus. 247, the two pieces make a mitered joint, Illus. 248.

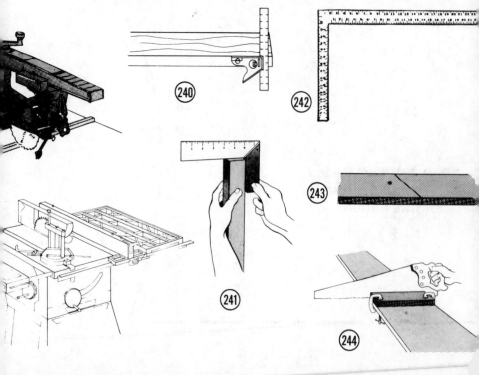

(240)

(242)

(243)

(241)

(244)

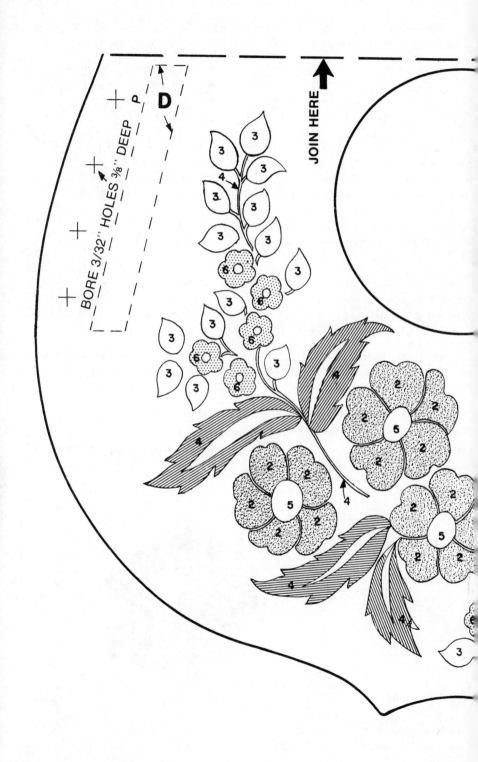

BORE 3/32" HOLES ⅜" DEEP

D

P

JOIN HERE

Doweling requires drilling holes in two pieces in exact position. Dowel centers, available in sets, Illus. 231, simplify locating matching holes.

These range from ¼, 5/16 to ⅜". Larger sizes are also available. For ¼" dowels, drill a ¼" hole. Place the ¼" dowel center in hole, Illus. 232. Carefully place the matching board in position against stop, Illus. 233. Press or tap lightly and the point marks matching part.

Always make a repair using same size lumber. Since size varied through the years, it's frequently necessary to "make" lumber to exact size. A case in point: If you need to replace a 1 x 2 that measured a full 1 x 2, you could, up to a short time ago, buy a 1 x 2 that measured ¾ x 1⅝". Today, 1 x 2 measures ¾ x 1½". If you need the full 1" thickness, cut a strip of ¼" plywood to length required. Glue or brad it to the 1 x 2, Illus. 234. If you need a full 2" width, buy a 1 x 3 and cut to size required.

All lumber contains "grain," direction of fibers. When cutting across grain, use a cross-cut saw, Illus. 235. When cutting with the grain, use a rip saw, Illus. 236; or an electric handsaw, Illus. 237; or table saw, Illus. 238; or radial arm saw, Illus. 239.

Before measuring length of a board, make certain end is square, Illus. 240. Use a try square, Illus. 241, or a framing square, Illus. 242. Place in position shown and draw a line square across the board.

Always draw a fine line. While a sharpened pencil will do it, a knife blade makes an even finer one.

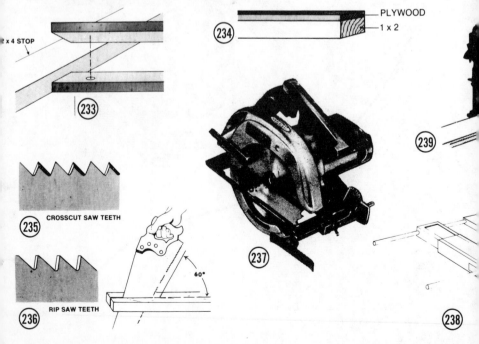

2 x 4 STOP

(233)

(234)

PLYWOOD
1 x 2

(239)

(235) CROSSCUT SAW TEETH

(237)

60°

(236) RIP SAW TEETH

(238)

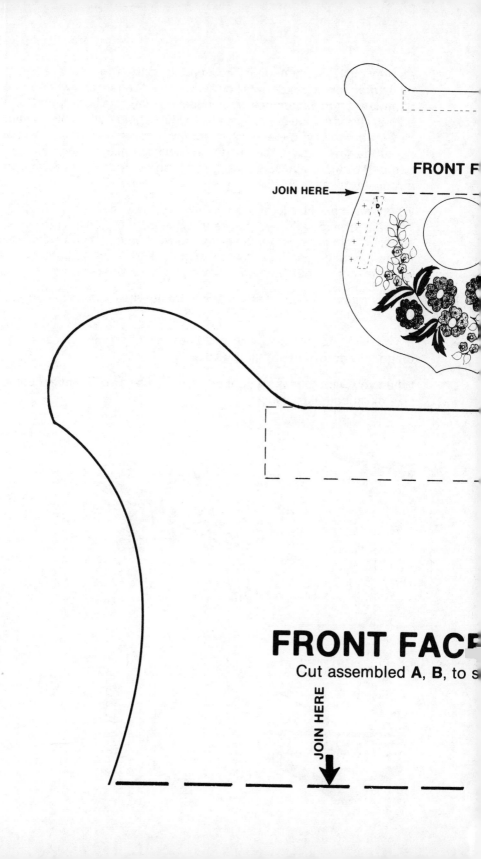

FRONT F

JOIN HERE→

D

FRONT FACE

Cut assembled **A, B**, to s

JOIN HERE

As previously mentioned, first test end of board with a square before measuring for length. Draw a line across face of board and where extra confidence and experience are needed, continue the line around both edges. This is a good policy since it provides a guide, Illus. 243, for your saw. Another way to make a straight cut is to use a miter box which keeps the saw blade perpendicular at all times while making a straight or mitered cut. Another sure way is to use an electric hand saw, table or a radial arm saw.

When making a butt joint, it's usually necessary to toenail, Illus. 246. Toenailing helps join two pieces in exact position. Toenail from the edge, or from the side whenever you do any framing. When toenailing framing lumber, use 8 penny common nails. Use two 16 penny nails when making a butt joint with 2 x 4's; 3 nails when nailing 2 x 6's.

Always replace a coping saw blade in frame with teeth pointing away from handle.

If you want to cut a board into equal width strips, place a rule diagonally across board, Illus. 249.

When you want to make a tight fitting joint, use a pen knife to outline size of rabbet, Illus. 250.

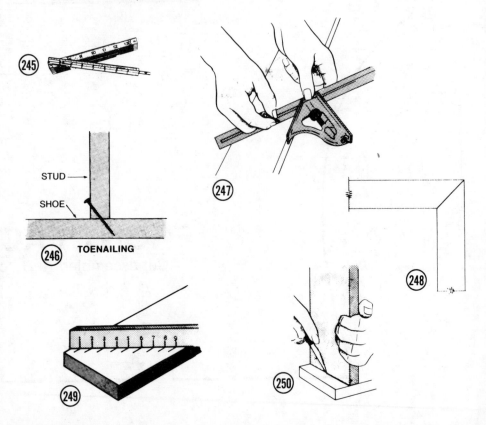

(245)

STUD

SHOE

(246) TOENAILING

(247)

(248)

(249)

(250)